MARK AND ANNA, MODELS

Mark and Anna, Models

reflections on the timeless wisdom
of Saint Augustine of Hippo
through the prism of postmodernity

GRACJAN KRASZEWSKI

AROUCA
PRESS

ISBN: 978-1-998492-43-5 (pbk)
ISBN: 978-1-998492-44-2 (hc)

Arouca Press
PO Box 55003
Bridgeport PO
Waterloo, ON N2J 0A5
Canada
www.aroucapress.com
Send inquiries to info@aroucapress.com

Contents

Dedication

for Kate

0.

Introductions and Framing
and Other Assorted Items

In December 2023 Arouca Press published my book of essays, *The Hippo Lectures*. Named in honor of our patron, Saint Augustine of _____, it was a book drawn from live audience talks that I have given monthly since September 2019 in my role as Director of Intellectual Formation at Vandal Catholic in Moscow, Idaho. Having to do a regular talk in front of real people is great preventive medicine for writer's block and good old-fashioned laziness. While *The Hippo Lectures* book was wide ranging—non-fiction reflections on politics, art, the climate, beer, et cetera, alongside two 'fiction intermissions'—I decided in the spring of 2024 to use the monthly talks for serialized story installments. Two Hippo Lectures in March and April of that year became the novella *Seraphim and the Dust Plague,* also published by Arouca Press.

Since this book you're holding in your hands is my fourth with Arouca Press—number three being my 900 page novel *Thermonuclear Mirth* (August, 2024)—and fourth in a row with them since my novel *The Holdout* appeared in 2018, followed by a Civil War history *Catholic Confederates* in 2020 (Adelaide Books and Kent State Univ. press, respectively), I'll beg your indulgence in allowing me to tell you, him, her, them, that guy, the other guy, and the whole world that Arouca Press is probably, and at least by my lights, the best publisher in North America and maybe on Planet Earth. I'm not saying this backed by any science, statistics, of even 'the science.' For who could design and then run appropriate tests to determine something like this anyways?

I'm saying Alex Barbas, editor in chief, will one day be spoken of in literary circles by way of that highest praise that encourages would be imitators to avoid imitation. 'My plan is to go to Los Angeles and wait tables and go to auditions and get my big break.' 'Please don't do that, be practical.' 'It worked for Brad Pitt.' 'You think *you're Brad Pitt?*' Future editors and book publishers will try to reach the grandeur and lofty heights Alex is currently taking Arouca Press only to be told, with an almost affectionate dismissiveness, perhaps even by way of a gentle pat on the head after being handed a warm plate of cookies and a glass of milk, 'I'm sorry, but you're no Alex Barbas.'

Maybe you prefer sports analogies. I love sports. Arouca Press compared to other publishers is like a boxing match where in the pre-fight lead up the latter is talking incessant trash, and has a great hype machine, and even gets into a scuffle at the weigh in but then during the fight Arouca Press just comes out from the opening bell landing punch after punch after punch after punch after punch until the referee has to stop the fight for the love of humanity and common decency too. Arouca Press is like a football team that has a 6'6 QB who can throw the ball 75 yards from his knees, and a fleet of sub 4.4 receivers, and a running back who somehow weighs 270 pounds but has 2% body fat and also runs not too far from a 4.5, but they prefer to beat opponents by giving it to their fullback (p.s. he's also jacked out of his mind, crazy fast, and borderline psycho, in a good way) on each play, just for the comedy. Because, when you think about it, it's hilarious to do nothing but a full back dive on each play and make it 2 and 2, first down, 2 and 3, first down, all the way down the field and then it's 35-0 at halftime well on the way to a 56-0 final score. That's Arouca Press in a nutshell. So, I hope you read my other books by them, and thank you for picking this one up, but do check out all their offerings in sum. They are wonderful. Thank you, for everything, Alex.

Equal thanks to the pastor at Saint Augustine's-Vandal Catholic, my friend, Father Chase Hasenoehrl, without whom the Hippo Lectures would have never come into being and then would never have become what they are and might yet still become. Thank you, Father Chase, and thank you to all the wonderful staff and people at Vandal Catholic. No one could ask for a more supportive, caring, and intelligent community (especially Andrew and Elizabeth Goeckner, whose introductions to these talks turned book chapters, listed in the last section -0.7, were as good, and as essential, as the talks themselves).

A heartfelt thanks to my wife, Kate, and my sons Søren and Bjørn; all my work is yours, for you, and made better by you. To my father, Charles: you're the best writer and man I know and to my mother, Aleksandra, you're a saint, and that you for a time taught a Russian language course at Penn State University in the early 1990s, not to too long after the wall had fallen, is very cool and even perfect; in terms of historical timing and all that. I could also thank my aunt Claire and my brother Konrad and his wife Colby and just go on and on and on but, suffice to say, I have a lot of people to thank for so many things and that in itself is a blessing.

Highest thanks, and all glory, to God, without whose grace I could do nothing, and to the Blessed Virgin Mary, my Queen, her most chaste spouse Saint Joseph, and all the angels and saints, you holy men and women of God, pray for us. The Benedictine monks of 6th century Europe had it right then and still do: *ora et labora,* prayer and work, there is nothing else, no other formulas or blueprint besides this. Do this and then get it done or don't do it and end up getting nothing done (of value, at least).

Closing, I'll come back to where I started. This book is not *The Hippo Lectures II*. Sequels, almost always, are bad. I still think the fact that *Napoleon Dynamite* never had a __

____ II: (something), is an unsung triumph of American cinematic history. Much like *Seraphim and the Dust Plague, Mark and Anna, Models* emerged FROM the Hippo Lectures monthly talks but IS NOT like *The Hippo Lectures* book in approach or style. So, what is *Mark and Anna* about, then?

First, it is a work wholly fictional. Even in the footnotes, you'll find fictional references alongside real ones.

Second, a work of postmodern fiction. You'll find plenty of different fonts, line breaks, uneven spaces, and colors throughout.

This because, third, it uses postmodern fiction and its experimental optics to present something very old and straightforward but sorely lacking in today's world: the lessons gleaned from the theology of Saint Augustine, a man, excepting Saint Thomas Aquinas, but maybe even if including him, who is perhaps the greatest mind the Church has yet seen. I have personally tried to do justice to the vast extent of Saint Augustine's thought, something impossible to cover *all* of but, nonetheless, that one can get through *a lot* of by leading an entire 'Year of Saint Augustine' class /reading group in my role as Director of Intellectual Formation at Vandal Catholic. Since Fall 2024, and planned through Spring 2025—September to May in the traditional academic semester format—I have gathered people from all walks of life to meet weekly and discuss *City of God, Confessions, On the Sermon on the Mount, On Christian Doctrine, On the Harmony of the Gospels, Trilogy on Faith and Happiness,* and much, much more.

Indeed, much more. I say with no small degree of satisfaction, and all glory to God for whatever good that has come of it, that Vandal Catholic's Year of Saint Augustine is quite possibly the longest treatment of the saint in all the world, all media formats considered. Many people, many of them much smarter than me, have done videos, perhaps even a series of videos, on Augustine.

Typically, these range in length from 20 minutes to a few hours.[1] We have done ten hours plus simply on *City of God*, and the entire Year of Saint Augustine will no doubt tally, in the final sum, fifty or maybe even sixty hours spanning roughly thirty individual episodes, some of them two hours in length. All of these can be watched on the YouTube Channel MapleGracjanSyrup under the playlist 'Maple Syrup History.'

Special thanks to regular attendees Loretta, George, Barb, Betsy (and Betsy's daughter, Erica, whose advice concerning Augustine from her own study of him proved invaluable in the planning phase of the course), Dominic, Nowrin and, of first order, a man named Brad whose last name is King and whose middle name should be, by order of the pope, changed and held in perpetuity as 'the.' Returning to books (and point 3 of the above—...it uses postmodern fiction and its experimental optics...), and this book you are and have been reading, there are plenty of books about Saint Augustine. I'm sure some are great and that some are terrible. I mentioned some of the good ones in the footnote above. None, at least as far as I know, try to amalgamate serious theological

---

[1] Much good work has been, and continues to be, done concerning Saint Augustine of Hippo. From the books side of things, the following would be a good place to start: Henry Chadwick's *Augustine of Hippo: A Life* (Oxford University Press, 2010) along with his *Augustine: A Very Short Introduction* (Oxford University Press, 2001), Rev. D. G. Hubert's *Sundays & Festivals with the Fathers of the Church: Homilies on the Gospels of the Ecclesiastical Year* (Waterloo, ON: Arouca Press, 2020), Bob and Penny Lord's *Saint Augustine and Saint Monica* (Journeys of Faith, 2009), and Peter Brown's *Augustine of Hippo: A Biography* (Berkeley, Univ California Press, 2013).

For those more inclined to videographic presentations, all of which are available of YouTube, please see Bishop Robert Barron's hour long 'A Life of Heroic Sanctity: Augustine of Hippo,' Father Casey Cole's nine minute primer, 'Saint You Should Know: Augustine of Hippo,' Sensus Fidelium's 'Saint Augustine (28 August)-Patron Saint of Theologians,' and Professor John Milbank's 'Why Study St Augustine of Hippo with John Milbank.'

points through the prism of a fun story that, at times, accelerates fun to hyper-absurd and maybe even insane.

There's a great flood that turns the prettiest dirt road in all of America to ice. There's lots of deadlifting and dunking. The president of the United States himself has to weigh in on a predicament late in the story. Idaho's Heyburn State Park and the Great Palouse Sea aka Lake Chatcolet, ever heard of them? Soon you will. While it is certainly a prose story, without question, there are 350 lines of poetry too, a sub-theme homage to Virgil's *Aeneid*.

Mark and Anna are at the center of it all. Mark and Anna are, as you'll find out, the best-looking people on Earth. Awash in a storm surge of hyperbole, where even mediocre meals get 5-star reviews, I assure you that I say this straight faced and as a matter of fact. People pass out and get injured at the mere sight of them. A grizzled old woman feels things in a toe she thought had been permanently damaged from a hammer decades ago upon meeting Mark. Another woman gets hit by a cement truck trying to run to him (she's okay, don't worry). The Governor of Tennessee threatens to shut down all public works in the state if Anna is not crowned Ms. Tennessee even though she is not from there. All the while, the two of them are led through a thorough lesson in Augustinian theology—this book's subtitle is, *reflections on the timeless wisdom of Saint Augustine of Hippo through the prism of postmodernity,* after all—by their spiritual advisor _____.[2]

It's long past time that fashion models got their due. They're people, too, with feelings and dreams and ambitions and favorite flavors of ice cream. God, ultimately He alone, can claim the at rest perfections of the Good, the True, and the Beautiful. While we humans fall short in all three categories, it is to models that we can look for the best of us in terms of beauty.

---

[2] you're going to have to read on and find out.

Thank you, models, for making it possible to dress, in a technical sense, like absolute trash by way of a ripped $2 hoodie, sixteen-hole sweatpants ($1.77), and lace less, coffee-stained Converses the thrift store gave you for free for you had already paid more than they had hoped for. If a guy or girl is good looking enough, it's not just cool, it becomes a trend. Thank you, models, for improving the effort output of society by anywhere from 16 to 28%. They see you, appreciate you, look at themselves, get depressed, but then think, there's hope, there's help, for while I maybe can never get to that level, I can actually shave off my gross beard, and make it to the gym more often than once a month, and google what type of shirt goes best with these types of pants. Thank you, by you just being you, making all of us better versions of ourselves.

Gracjan Kraszewski
Pullman, the Palouse, Washington,
7 miles from where one can find Vandal Catholic,
Moscow, the Palouse, Idaho,
(because it really is all about that city-state, cloud ringed, rich soil kingdom called 'the Palouse')
20 January,[3] AD 2025

---

[3] Feast of Saint Sebastian, patron saint of athletes, soldiers, the disabled, the plague stricken, and Cusco, Peru.

the City of God v. the City of Man

'Sure, thank you,' she says, confirming that she would like a cup of coffee on the side. The waiter smiles and walks away.

He had ordered crème brûlée.

She, mini chocolate cake.

It's not typical to share dessert on a first date and tonight had proceeded as such. What the future might hold, if anything at all, was unknown. It was too early to tell.

She ordering coffee along with dessert was a positive sign, he thought. It was a strong indicator of a person's underlying character. People who order coffee with dessert—even half past ten in the evening, as it was now, the sun having set hours ago, hardly noticeable for the rain obscuring it then had kept on coming down, hard, pelting the thin-paned windows of this side alley boutique where the two of them had been given a handsome corner table, flowers on the table, lit candles, the whole place illuminated solely by candlelight, that was a theme, and the food had been not bad and the service good and now it had just about come to an end, the whole night, maybe the whole thing, and he and she had both ordered coffee along with their dessert—probably appreciate classical music, they most likely take care to get regular exercise, they like large dogs, maybe Rottweilers best of all, take the time to learn a foreign language, and most likely do not like superhero movies, pop music, mindfulness, and apps that you can download or upload onto your phone.

They might not even own a phone, who knows.

He didn't know if she did or did not own a phone.

No technology was also one of this restaurant's requirements. At this stage he was not yet ready to ask her for
her number, so he didn't know if she owned or did not
own a phone. Maybe after the coffee he'd do it, ask her.
When she got back, maybe then, for she was momentarily
gone. After thanking the waiter, she had excused herself
and followed him back towards the bar.

He turns his head and sees them talking, she gesturing
with her hands, explaining something. It looks like she's
ordering him about, he thinks, laughing. She seems to be
commanding him regarding the way the milk must be
whipped, that she wants honey, real honey, not imitation
sweetener, and it should be poured in and mixed such as
this and that and he can't help feeling his attraction to her
build by the second. It's like he's a total idiot and it doesn't
matter that he works here, she is the Empress of the Evening Coffee slow sipped under a steady rain and it will be
this way by my Imperial Edict. It's great, it's wonderful.

That the date was typical does not mean it was bad.
Okay plus, at minimum, but most likely good, yes, he
assures himself, she probably wouldn't have ordered that
coffee it she didn't feel the same way. Good for sure. The
no technology thing was good. They had talked freely
and easily the whole night. About their former shared
profession, the reason they're here in the first place, about
SEC football, the pros and cons of RV camping in late
September, this relative to *what if you like to paddle board on
the lake but is the lake going to be too cold then(?)*, and about the
best type of postmodern art,[1] and playlists for a long road
trip, and sisters, and motels in the Memphis, Tennessee
general, geographical region.

So, yeah, good, it had been good, definitely good. He
turns his head. She's still up there. Now, to the real

---

[1] Toilet on wall vs. I dipped my head in paint and headbutted a wall
were the finalists, but they had not reached a consensus.

question, the answer was a resounding yes. Most beautiful woman he had ever seen. Most beautiful woman ever. And he was quite good looking himself, no doubt. They had met on the dating site formermodelsneedlongtermlovetoo.edu

.edu because the University of Idaho had taken a particular interest in what a sociology professor called 'the silent epidemic of single models.' 'Former models,' he explained in a wide-ranging interview to the *Seattle Times*, 'are too good looking. People, I mean non-models, are often intimidated to even speak with them. Models soon fall into a vicious cycle of detachment and isolation. I sincerely believe this is the next public health crisis. No, it's already upon us. It's in the public interest that we fix this, and fast, and that public funds and the best minds apply themselves to it. Serious discussions were held as to perhaps making it .gov, as a few proposals argued it was a matter of national security. But, yes, .com, no, that will not do.'

They had both signed up.

They matched.

They were flown out here, to this restaurant located in a region called

the Palouse,

a land of rolling hills and fertile fields and late summer sunsets almost as attractive as they are, to a restaurant hidden on a dirt road off a main dirt road called

the Old Moscow Pullman Highway.

Down this first, hidden dirt road are a few buildings, on something like a side street, a side alley, and here is this, and here they are, and it has not stopped raining, and she has not yet returned.

Good looking?

The both of them?

No question. He worked for Gucci for three years and then did a rather regrettable ten-month stint as the front man for an experimental Icelandic cologne. One photo shoot required him to stand barefoot on an ice shelf. It was supposed to take half an hour, but it lasted half a day, and he'd rather just not talk about it. His good looks have something like national absurdity tied to them. You've all heard the story. How he was walking downtown in his small hometown one day and one woman was so taken by his appearance she dropped her groceries and sprinted across the street towards him and was hit in the middle of the street by another woman who was operating a cement truck but had also been completely distracted by the sight of this man walking.

You've all seen the local newspaper's headline from that day. The one the *New York Times* called 'unforgivably callous and cruel;' the *Los Angeles Times,* 'evidence that flyover country should remain as such until the end of time.' The *Miami Herald* opined, 'bigotry is alive and well today, and it seems the dumber the practitioner, the more refined the product.'

8

THE TWO DUMB BIMBOS OF BROAD STREET; or, WHY
WOMEN SHOULD NEVER OPERATE VEHICLES OR DO ANY-
THING OF CONSEQUENCE IN PUBLIC, a brief tragedy in one act.
—'Why in the son of a b**** f*** is there any longer a debate
about whether women should vote, drive cars, own property, speak
in public. . . .

Please see: BIMBOS, A3.

MADISON CENTRAL DEFEATS HIGH COUNTY, 42–7.

'. . .

Please see: LOCAL SPORTS, B2

LOOKING FOR GARDENING TIPS THIS FALL? TRY THESE EASY
TO IMPLEMENT RECOMMENDATIONS FROM OUR EXPERT
ON SITE.

'. . .

Please see: HOME & HEARTH, C3

DOCTORS SAY LOCAL MAN LUCKY TO BE ALIVE AFTER STUNT
GONE WRONG. 'I BASICALLY TRIED TO DRINK TWO GALLONS
OF DONKEY URINE SHOTGUN STYLE AND I REGRET IT.'

'. . .

Please see: HORSING AROUND, A8

STORM CELL FROM WEST 'MOST LIKELY WILL PASS US BY,'
METEROLOGISTS CLAIM.

'. . .

Please see: LOCAL WEATHER, D5

Luckily, she was okay, the woman hit by the cement truck. It was just a light bump, dislocated hip, nothing more serious than that. Three months of physical therapy and she was right as rain. But you remember the embarrassing rest of the story, right? How when the mayor asked this man to, please, no longer show his face in public, for he really was *that* good looking, she concluded by asking him to consider dating her niece. 'She's a great girl, you'd love her. 24, graduated from Oklahoma State with a degree in kinesiology two years ago. She's very nice, a great baker... I'm sorry,' she said, catching herself mid faux pas. 'I'm sorry, never mind.'

She, the fellow model, his date, still telling that waiter something about the coffee, still, poor guy, she's really putting him through it now, she has had similar experiences. Maybe the University of Idaho is spot on creating this program. Who can understand a former model better than a former model? Maybe the University is on to something, maybe that sociologist is right. She herself had worked five years as a model and in the center of all, mid-town Manhattan, signed after a fierce bidding war between three agencies all of whom were somewhere in the single digits when it came to the 'best of' 'the top 10,' that kind of thing. Before that, while in her early 20s, she had been named Miss Alabama twice and Miss Tennessee three times. The latter crown was not without controversy.

Born in Montgomery, she had grown up in Mobile and Gulf Coast Texas, and attended school in Tuscaloosa, having hardly ever set foot in Tennessee. Both times she won Miss Alabama it was determined, and here's the citation issued on official government letterhead out of some office in Nashville, that she was 'clearly, head and shoulders, far above the available candidates in our state [2] and that justice requires she be crowned, even in absentia.'

---

2 Tennessee.

Her Tennessee three-peat was most controversial at all. She was already then living in New York, out of this game anyways, but the governor of Tennessee threatened to withhold all public funds to the universities and, quote, 'let all the bridges fall over and the potholes get as big as the craters on the moon if our girl isn't recognized as the rightful Queen of Tennessee.' A compromise was eventually reached: the universities got their funding, potholes were filled and creaking bridges reinforced, and she was crowned Miss Tennessee, again.

Now,

finally,

she's back.

He stands and pushes his chair in because he's ready to take this to the next level, to lay his heart bare and tell her how he's feeling and—

'Excuse me—

He turns to his left and looks. Wait…, 'what?—

'Excuse me,' the gruff voice says again, this man, standing, an old man, hair all white, posture stooped, rough beard but a nice moustache, blue slacks, well faded, wearing a handsome dress shirt buttoned all the way to the top save for the final button. He looks like an Irish sheep herder who plays the fiddle at the pub on weekends.

'Do the two of you want to make this night truly special?' he asks, now standing in between him and her and, *you know, thanks, man, thanks a lot, bro. She had been gone for a million years and I finally worked up the courage and now, you, you.*

'Here,' he says, pulling a small, sea-green book out from somewhere and placing it on the table. The title reads,

The City of God

The author,
someone named
'Saint Augustine.'

'It's a simple as this,' he says, looking back between him and her and motioning at both of them. 'It's as simple as this: there is a heavenly City of God, Christ's Holy Bride, His Church on Earth against which the gates of hell, as everyone knows, shall not prevail, and this leading into the eternal, eternity as not endless time but the absence of it, City of God in Heaven, the Beatific Vision beheld by the Blessed Virgin Mary, all the angels and saints, all you holy men and women of God, pray for us, and we should be about that in our daily lives:

the city of God.

By God's grace choose that, not, the other option: the fallen, City of Man, filled to the brim, often overflowing with all its avarice, angers, lusts and constant lust for domination that, if left unchecked, if not conquered by the City of God, here and now on Earth, I mean, for the eternal victory has already been won once and for all on Calvary, if left unchecked, this City of Man leads into an eternal option too, that worst of all bad options, bad option

hell.

So,' he says, motioning once and yet again, 'do you want to take a little walk and I'll talk and you can listen and learn and then later start living this, I mean *do* these things in your life?'

He, the male model, says nothing. He doesn't know about all this. He just wants to tell this girl he's probably in love with her and then this guy shows up and—...

'Yes' she says. 'We'll go with you,' smiling more at him, the male model, than at the old guy. Her smile puts him, the male model, into a better mood by at least 2 or maybe even 300% and just like that, instantaneously.

'Excellent,' the old man says. 'First, what are your names?'

'Anna.'

'Mark.'

'I'm L.K,' the man says, shaking their hands in turn. 'LeBron Kobe McShaunessaey. You can just call me LeBron. Once upon a time I wrote a book about Saint Augustine myself,' pulling out a blue covered, well-worn hardcover, the back cover nearly completely detached. He taps on it twice and hands it to Anna.[3] She flips it over twice and opens it one time before handing it to Mark who just stares at it before handing it back to LeBron. 'However long our talking and, well, however long our interactions, I guess, last, rest assured that my main sources of advice-dispensation will be Augustine's *City of God,* his *Confessions,* and, also, my very own *Interconnected Web-Currents.* So, what we're going to do is simple. We're going to walk outside and sit down on some wet lentil hill and I'm going to

---

[3] LeBron Kobe McShaunessaey, *The Interconnected Philosophical, Theological, and Super-Syntaxstructural Web-Currents of Saint Augustine of Hippo's Thought, Speeches, and Writings in a Triple Comparative Optic-Light lens reflected through the 4th, 5th, and 20th centuries: a compilation of quotes, insights, and out the box hyperspeculative non straw man argumentation.* (New York: William Marcus & Sons, 1997), 598 pps.*

*—upon publication the William M & S style guide encouraged academics who would use this book, its 43 word title the longest they had published by 35 words, to abbreviate-cite the work as such:

LeBron Kobe McShaunessaey, *The Interconnected Web-Currents of Saint Augustine of Hippo's Thought.*

explain this book to you—I mean *City of God,* we'll begin there—and I mean reduce it down its most fundamental elements, and quick, and then you can go and, like I said, live it. It's basically like this.

There are three features of the City of Man, the bad stuff, and I want you to avoid them. Bad stuff that corrodes the soul, breaks you down and reduces you, even if first slowly, into a shell of yourself multiplied by many shells until one day you wake up and you're right there, standing on the precipice of hell itself.

1. Gossip and calumny and a refusal to mind one's own business.
2. Cringy political caricatures
3. Putting hope in earthly princes, which is the ultimate building your house on sand, not stone thing

...do you understand?'

Anna was nodding so Mark did the same. Maybe Anna really did understand and agree. Mark did not understand so he could not agree or disagree and all he was thinking about anyways was how good Anna looked in her jacket and now that they were outside, in the cool night air, that he wished LeBron would disappear, just go away back to whence he had come because although he did not have a ring, and nothing close to that, he wanted to get down on a knee and ask her a question but LeBron was sadly not gone, rather, worse, he was leading them onto that soft lentil hill just outside the restaurant, like he said he would, and he motioned for them to sit down and they did and wow, Anna really was truly, unbelievably beautiful and that at least mitigated, low heat simmer reduced, even if only a little bit, his anger at LeBron for interrupting them before and for now, this, whatever this was.

The hill was wetter than Mark had anticipated and now firmly plotted down into the Palouse soil his thoughts had shifted and he could only think one thing:

I really hate LeBron.

'First,' LeBron says, standing over them, almost shouting. *Oh, cool,* Mark thought, *cool, great. He gets to stand, dry. We have to sit on the ground.*

'First, avoid gossip and calumny and mind your own business. Saint Augustine said: "love God and then do whatever you want.[4]" What he meant was, if a person is putting God first, living that first commandment, and so therefore will be loving his neighbor as himself, and keeping all the commandments besides, just leave them alone. After that, following those, there is no way to the Father but through Christ absolutes, it's a lot of relative stuff. There is

---

[4] McShaunessaey, *The Interconnected Web-Currents of Saint Augustine of Hippo's Thought*, 226.

18

no
best profession,
best ice cream,[5]
best way to dress,
best hobby,
best reading group set-up,
best flowers to put in your garden,
best time to water your garden, so on and so forth. Not enough people ever hear, and take to heart, this great advice:

just shut up and mind your own business.

---

[5] Actually, there is: mint chocolate chip.

City of God stuff?

Minding your own business and making the most of your talents.

Augustine loved the Bible, loved the Gospels. You should too. Instead of worrying about what your neighbor is doing, first, shut up,

second, stop,

third, go read the parable of the talents in Matthew 25 and realize God is going to ask you:

" what have you done with the gifts I gave you?"

He's not going to ask you, "what time did your neighbor decide to mow his lawn?" Shut up, mind your own business, get to making the most of your gifts and glorifying God. That's City of God behavior that leads to happiness now and forever. But people, we all of us fallen, so wounded, so open, our concupiscent sores, we love the City of Man. So we do mind others business, criticize relentlessly all they do, those closest to us perhaps most, annoying them worst of all, and waste our talents by wasting our time worrying about others, and commit sin, sin, so much sin—see the Catechism if you don't believe me, which condemns, in no uncertain terms calumny (lying about others to others) and detraction (making public others' faults)[6]—so much sin by just talking trash about others and all the time. If you want to find out if you're more in the City of God or the City of Man, ask yourself: "do I promote, seek out, and deeply enjoy gossip, or no?" When you've answered that, you'll have your answer.'

---

6 *The Penny Catechism: A Catechism of Christian Doctrine* (Approved by the Archbishops and Bishops of England and Wales, and Directed to be Used in all their Dioceses, Charlotte, NC: TAN Books, 2012), No. 221, 35.

Mind your own business, Mark thinks to himself, what a
hypocrite, LeBron. I mean he walked right into our business, just about destroying all my dreams, all my hope of
love, but . . . wait . . . wait . . . his thoughts stop cold as he
notices Anna, who was sitting about three feet from him
on this cold wet hill, has now scooted . . . → . . . → . . . →
towards him and, wait, *happiness I might just pass out, black out,*
he thinks looking down, ↓

↓

↓

                she's . . . we're almost like,
                [(huddling together)]
                or something, oh man . . .

LeBron breaks in, as he seems wont to do, with

'Second, avoid the very City of Man cringy political
caricatures. There are too many of them to count so
I'll keep it brief. !!!***Note to morons:***!!! this presidential or gubernatorial candidate you swear is the next
King David, or Queen Katharine of Aragon, or worse
of all, Batman or something, some kind of superhero
riding in to rid whatever problems your "Gotham City"
is afflicted with, they're not, also they suck, also, they are
probably liars, also, probably they got into this whole
business because they want to do interviews, meaning
be on TV, wear expensive clothes, feel like they matter, because we all want that. Augustine himself will tell
you that disordered desire for popular acclaim is very
much a part of our fallen condition too,[7] it's not just the

---

[7] McShaunessaey, *The Interconnected Web-Currents of Saint Augustine of
Hippo's Thought,* 17.

leaders, all of us suffer from this but, yes, look,' LeBron says, pausing as he taps on his teal copy of the *City of God*. 'Look, be involved in politics. Augustine, Aquinas, Pope Leo XIII, Pope St Pius X, all of them call us to make Christ more present in our societies, for sure. As Augustine says in this book: without a transcendent principle, the City of Man will become more and more man, more fallen, so, yes, !!!***note to Catholics and people of good will***!!!: participate, vote, maybe even run for office if you're called to it. But can you please—and with this we'll know you aspire to citizenship in the City of God—just be like "I'm voting for ___because he is the lesser of two evils compared to ___. I'm voting for ___ because she , overall, better represents my values than ____." That's it, simple and without the "I'm voting for ____ because he's amazing and he's going to change everything, he's like a medieval knight mixed with an ancient Greek king like Pericles and he's so wise and so"... because,' LeBron says, huffing, and now both Anna and Mark can tell how worked up he's getting, 'because when I hear City of Man stuff like that I go off the handle, even to myself; interiorly, I mean. Outside I'm smiling, trying to be polite. Inside it's:

please no,

no, no, no,

no,

    please stop, stop, please,

no,

no,

no,

where is a big thick branch, a stick?

No,

no,

no, please, no, no, no, no, please no, no, please, no, no, either shut up or just

beat me with this stick over and over
and over over over over over over
and over
again

because that would be more tolerable than this. And
this—cringy political caricatures—lead into
third,
and finally,
the final marker of the City of Man:

putting hope in
earthly princes.

This one is con-
nected to, and flows from, the second. Those who frame
any candidate in the most florid praises and imagine him
or her as the solution to so many ills, having declared
this in cringy caricature, will soon graduate to building
edifices of imagined grandness around them until you
get, sure, maybe far down the road, but frog in boiling
water, the Stalin-like or Mao-like titles of deferential syco-
phantism. The leader you exaggerate and then drool over
will repay your service by giving you what you actually
want, what your actions have clearly bespoken: a total and
complete tyranny over you and yours. And then, finally,'
Lebron says, now holding his index finger up and waving
it side to side, 'finally comes the great punchline here.
The person
fails.
Because people
fail,
even the grandest princes
fail,
for they are not God, sand not stone is what
all of them build with but as for you, choose stone,[8]

---

[8] Please see: the conclusion to Christ's Sermon on the Mount (Mt.,
chapters 5-7) in chapter 7 of Saint Matthew's Gospel.

build your house, your politics, your all on Christ and His Church. Now, that, that's City of God stuff and we should be about that; and as often and as much as is possible...would you like a quick recap?'

Mark can say nothing at the moment. He has, and maybe for the first time ever, glimpsed true happiness. Sometime something like 30 seconds ago, or maybe 45, who's counting, Anna had eliminated all the distance between them

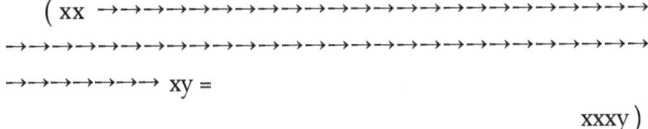

(xx →→→→→→→→→→→→→→→→→→→→→→→→ →→→→→→→→→→→→→→→→→→→→→→→→→ →→→→→→→→ xy =

xxxy)

and just wrapped her arm around his arm, cuddled up and next to him →→→ properly, dropped her head onto

↓

↓

his shoulder—it was still there, on his shoulder, and so now he knew, Mark did, and at that precise moment, yes, 100%: the date must have gone really, really good. Her hair smelled like an alpine forest after two inches of early winter snow, and her eyes were as deep and clear as Flathead Lake, and her smile, her ears, even her earlobes were of a beauty beyond compare. Mark burst out into song.

A, B, C, D, eeeee, F, G!

Aych, eyeeee, J, K, L, m, enno, P!

Q R S, Tee, U—

'Mark, what are you doing?' Anna asks.

'Oh-sorry...,' for so transfixed had he been he had not noticed he had been singing out loud.

'What was that?' LeBron says. 'Are you okay?'

'Yep, mhmm. I'm good, yep.'

'So like I was saying,' LeBron continues, 'would you like a recap of what I just told you?'

Mark couldn't care less about anything, *whatever, LeBron, whatever, dude, sure, go for it*. Anna squeezes his arm and cuddles even closer and says,

'We'd love a recap.'

'Excellent,' LeBron says. 'Remember the advice of Saint Augustine and these three tips. It's like the seven vices and their corresponding virtues; avoid pride, be humble; avoid lust, be chaste.... Okay?'

Mark and Anna nod.

'Avoid the first City of Man pitfall, 1. Gossip and calumny and a refusal to mind one's own business. Instead, don't worry about your neighbor at all, except to pray for him and wish him well and help him if he needs help when you can help. Minding your own business will mean minding the things, especially the talents, God has given you to serve Him, and others, and be happy yourself. Be about those, City of God things.

Avoid pitfall, 2. cringy political caricatures, instead vote your conscience and vote for a better world, now and forever, but know it's just that: a vote, you did your part, great, but the things of this passing world are indeed ever passing. Heaven and Earth will pass away but my Word will not pass away,[9] amen. Therefore, participating in politics minus anything more will serve God and man all the better, will put a little more City of God into the City of Man and, finally, this attitude will keep you safe from City of Man pitfall, 3. putting hope in princes. If

---

[9] Luke 21:33.

you've made it this far in the advice ledger and kept true to the path I've laid out for you, I know you'll only put your hope, your final hopes, in Christ and nothing else. Praise God. Now,' LeBron says, throwing the book high into the night sky and catching it, quite athletically, on the way down, 'what would you like to do? What now?'

Mark doesn't hesitate. 'I wanna marry Anna.'

What happened next is to be filed under the truth is stranger than fiction files for sure. If it didn't really happen, you wouldn't believe it, but it did, and here it is told in the simplest and most straightforward way possible. For sometimes just the facts, thank you very much, is the best way to tell the story.

As soon as Mark said,

'I want to marry Anna,'

Anna jumped up and put a ring on her own finger and said to him,

'I'll take that as a proposal. My answer is yes.'

She proceeded to explain to him that she had been talking to the bartender for so long before because *where was that ring by the way(?)*, but he had finally found it, and that's when she had come back to their table. She told him that prior to their date, here, tonight on the Palouse—thank you, formermodelsneedlongtermlovetoo.edu

—Anna had seen some of his modeling photos from the Iceland Fjord fashion shoot and she had resolved, from the first shot, 'I will marry this man one day if it's the last thing I do.' Hearing that, Mark wanted to call Iceland, the whole country, and just express his gratitude. Burt then, wait, Mark said, we can't just do this because we need a priest. LeBron smiled and informed them he was in fact

Father LeBron Kobe McShaunssaey, OSB

Fr. Lebron told them to walk a little further into the night and right over a hill there was a church, and it was packed full with guests, all models, waiting for Mark and Anna and this seemingly impromptu wedding, that to this point, was going off like planned and prepared for years in advance. So, think about that: most weddings have people, guests, who are

Class 1: good looking, and
Class 2: it depends on your type, and
Class 3-4: beauty is in the eye of the beholder, and
Class Undefined/Unranked: if you don't have something nice to say don't say anything at all.

But these guests, being all models,

[10],

---

[10] Class 0 level: class, wow.

meant it was by far the best-looking wedding in all of human history.

Whether Mark and Anna are happy now, like happily ever after or not, who knows? I don't know, I don't know if they're happy or not; I hope they are. I am sure about this one thing: if you become friends with them, never, ever find yourself in a photo with them. I want you to be happy too, believe me, and if you and your spouse or significant other find yourself in a photo alongside them and you see it, your self-esteem is going to take a significant pummeling, an old school, West Texas[11] beatdown beating. Have a good and high sense of self-worth? Well, you used to anyways. Don't do that to yourself, care to avoid that, avoid City of Man things, seek the City of God, and be assured that seeking first the Kingdom of God, and His righteousness, God will give you all good things besides.[12]

That's what Father LeBron wrote in his journal. His most recent entry. That immediately preceding paragraph, those 150 words. He was hoping to see them again, soon. *To their health,* he said, aloud, to no one. He raised a glass of beer and clinked it against a mug of beer he had just poured.

Then, he drank.

---

[11] FYI (as mentioned earlier and here yet again, in recall fashion): Anna had lived in Corpus Christi, TX for two years in her youth* in between the all-Alabama born in Montgomery "grew up" as in see: spent the significant majority of her formative years, in Mobile. But so East/ South Texas, Gulf Coastal Texas, not West Texas here; Corpus Christi.

*grandparents; paternal side.

[12] Matthew 6:33

2.

the Problem of Evil

I sing of good looks and of a man, a woman: their fate[13]
had not exactly made them fugitive, for even those possessed of the
highest beauty are not the first
to journey from paycheck to paycheck, enormous payouts ensuring
their commitments. But the loneliness
in the meantime
        between.
The meaninglessness that maybe all this
means.
Anna and Mark had long ago resolved
would that even the coasts of old Troy as far as Italy and the Lavinian
shores come calling
no,
we are done,   12
we are no longer models,
we have done our time,
and now time, until the end of our times, will be our time,
passed together in hopeful drawn out lazy summer sunsets under
creaking oaks,
gently swaying in a light breeze wholly apart   17
it,
from foreboding meteorological portends
us,   20
from that, modeling, all
that.   22

When last we heard of our heroes
and the perpetual vows that bound them,
Father LeBron calling down blessings from on high while a crowd
not much less good looking

---

13 Please see: Virgil, *The Aeneid* (New York: Bantam Dell, 1971. trans.
Allen Mandelbaum), Book I, 1.

than them
looked on,   27
we parted company, perhaps into the dreamy land of memories fading
ever steadily into recollections
ever hazier, we, yes, us too decline we eventually all do,
and if not you, then I,
and she and he too
wondered: would they achieve that elusive happily ever after?   33

Call no man happy before the day
of his death, as the Holy Book[14]
says. Mark and Anna yet live. Hopefully laughter and play

and seeing their children and children's children[15] remains in store
for them. Look,
a long life is still ahead, God willing, so,
ever after? Much too early to say. But cook

thyself well done I beg thee bid thyself not. Thy head in thought
pretzel knots slappy,   40
sappy and mushy undo. Assuredly, I tell you in the plainspoken truth,
rather rest assured:

O, they've been happy. It's been good, very good, so far.   42

Mark: That lake is 60,000 feet deep.
Anna: No.   44
Mark: Yes.
She: No, nuh uh, no way.
—Yes.
—Nuh uh, baby, stop. No way! Nu uh, no, no it's not.
—Yes.
—.... No.   50
—Yep.
—Baby! No it's not, please stop it! Stop, no way!
—Yes.   53

---

[14] Sirach 11:28–30.
[15] Psalm 128:6.

It went on that like for a while. They were having so much fun. Mark and Anna were standing on the teal colored, ridiculously gorgeous—how appropriate, that—Great Idaho Bridge which can transport one across the Great Palouse Sea, also known as Lake Chatcolet, 5 miles east of Plummer, Idaho, looking down, laughing, hugging, she sometimes playfully slapping him on the arm, loving life.

They were on their honeymoon, here at Heyburn State Park, 8 miles from Saint Marie's, ID but now in the other direction.[16] Although staying at the Benewah Lake campground—putting extra logs on the campfire with attention to detail so as to keep it burning long past what most would aspire to, getting a second smores made before a third became a fourth—they had swam enough at Rocky Point to have swallowed at least a gallon of lake water, and had biked to Harrison for soft serve ice cream with sprinkles on top, and been a top this bridge, the Great Idaho Bridge, each and every day of their weeklong stay.

They did all these things in between doing that which most people do most on their honeymoon. They did a lot of that. Both Mark and Anna had 'waited for marriage.' No big deal, each kind of subliminally, sub-consciously thought. Of course, of course you wait to do that only after very serious, lifelong vows, and the trust and security that comes with that to compensate for the radical vulnerability and strangeness and uniqueness of it all. Neither of them had or would ever talk about it, 'waiting,' at least not often and never publicly. Those things were best lived and shut up about. Talking about all that, in whatever fashion, was pathetic. But, yes, they had both been raised as Catholics—and had kept to that faith throughout their

---

[16] West (of Saint Marie's, thereby placing Heyburn SP in between Plummer and Saint Marie's with Coeur d'Alene but some 30 minutes plus north for Lake Chatcolet is, in the cartographical big picture, the very southern tip of Lake Coeur d'Alene).

lives, making sure to make it to Sunday Mass even when shooting in the most remote locations, having something like a daily prayer life, at times rich, other times dry, but there nonetheless, at minimum some prayers at waking and before going to bed, and Anna had long ago adopted the habit of daily Bible reading, even just ten or fifteen minutes or so, and, come to think of it, that was a question on the 32 question match-questionnaire from formermodelsneedlongtermlovetoo.edu, something about religion—and had internalized however imperfectly the morals and mores therein throughout their lives right up to that first date and it had never occurred to either of them to violate this withholding for any reason save the Matrimonial stamp of approval. So, when on that first date, they broached this subject (before Anna had left for that long stay up at the bar pre-desserttime coffee) and found themselves on equal footing, it certainly moved things forward and fast. The honeymoon at Heyburn State Park had been something like making up for lost time, it was great.

But, all in all, it was check in that made all the difference and shattered the best of their intentions concerning photographic, photogenic, retirement.

'I'm sorry, um,' the woman at the park headquarters said, fanning herself with a *Welcome to Heyburn State Park!* brochure. 'Can you please, can you, um, can you take your parking pass and please go, please.'

This woman's assistant, Delaney, had fainted a literal 2.8 seconds after seeing Mark walk through the door. Mark had forgotten what the sight of his face, when shown without warning, could do. People in the modeling world, being around beautiful people on a regular basis, had developed a tolerance, a type of immunity, if you will. Not so for the normal and uninitiated. Poor Delaney, she never stood a chance. It's certainly not her fault. 20 years old, U of I Forestry and Natural Resources major, landed this awesome summer gig at Heyburn state park. She's just trying to do her job, she likes dogs, she's just trying to help people out, she loves historical fictions and her sisters, she's just trying to input license plate numbers and length of stay into the computer, Delaney, and in walked Mark and she hardly had time to process the thought on the forefront of her mind—*best looking guy I have ever…*—before she slumped in her seat and fell off the chair onto the floor, out cold.

'Please,' the woman said, now shielding her eyes with the brochure. 'We can't call the paramedics to resuscitate her and then do all the health checks until the two of you leave. We can't have people dropping like flies at the sight of you two. I will say,' still shielding her eyes, 'I, this is actually, this is actually funny, because I honestly cannot believe the two of you are this good looking. Huh, tens marry tens, right? Ha! What are the both of you? Five hundred thirty threes? Ha! I need you to leave. I'm a tough old bird, I'm one of those Idaho women who likes to shoot guns, and ride horses, and chop down trees with axes the axes pressing into my flesh that look, see here, look at the callouses on my hands, I've got callouses on my hands like a Bulgarian powerlifter. I've got forearms like a Texas outback oil rig operator. My face is weather-beaten beyond belief and, trust me, I'm tough as nails, hard as granite, and yet you,' pointing at Mark, 'you're still getting to me. Look, my eyes are watering. My left toe is tingling and I haven't felt that foot since I dropped a hammer on it back in '78. I need you to leave. Please.'

Mark and Anna turned to leave. Anna, relieved, that while Delaney was still lying there, on the cold floor, she was visibly breathing and looked to be doing fine besides.

'Wait . . .' the woman said, 'before you go, can I, can I, I, . . . get a photo? A photo of the two of you?'

Mark and Anna obliged and they were happy to oblige and that is, rather now looking back, was, the aforementioned shattering of the best of their intentions concerning photographic, photogenic, retirement. Mark and Anna, the two of them individually, but all the more so together, like to model, they really do. Modeling for the sake of modeling, for love of the game, and the two of them standing there, rather posing there, arm in arm in the Heyburn State Park Welcome center as the front desk woman snapped a few photos on her long needing to be updated iPhone, convinced them to come out of retirement and do one more photo shoot; together.

This one photo shoot[17] became a North American tour,[18] and it was extremely well-received, and they made more money from this three month tour than they had in the entirety of their previous, also very well paid, careers. But then Mark really got into reading the Desert Fathers and read how St Anthony of Egypt[19] had heard a sermon

---

[17] South Pacific Surf: The New Tropical Fragrance from Andrew Benjamin.

[18] Promoted as 'Mark and Anna March and Model across Canada and the U.S.: The Conquest Tour.' Stops in Calgary, AB, Los Angeles, CA, and Fargo, ND sold out in less than 10 minutes.

[19] Could he be any more based? P.s. he also lived to be 105 years old. (AD 251–356).

on Christ's instructions to the rich young man about (a) keep the commandments, (b) sell what you have and give to the poor, and (c) come, follow Me,[20] and so while they did not sell ALL they had, they did give away a lot, and in a true love your neighbor as yourself for the sake of loving God spirit,[21] and then, following all this, resolved to do two things:

1. Buy a lake house near the shores of the Great Palouse Sea.
  &
2. Contact Father Lebron.

And so, they did;   54
         &   55
      they did.   56

---

[20] Matthew 19:16–22.
[21] Matthew 22:36–40.

38

Father LeBron,
It's me, Mark,
and I've know it's been a while, we've been long gone

from your thoughts, your view. Stark
can be the life unguided by a spiritual advisor, see,
although, confess I must, happy as a lark   62

Anna and me,
have found, and do find,   64
ourselves to be.

But, Father LeBruh: I think this time blind
I am not in the ways of self-deception or the lack
of self-knowledge. We're done, modeling. Most kind
to us you would be, your counsel like from the desert sky manna,
if you'd consent us to shepherd, ya boy, Mark, that girl, my wife, Anna.

                                                             70

Father LeBron called them back and left an old school please leave your message after the tone voicemail that was breathlessly without punctuation and explained, verbatim, 'Guys yes of course I've been thinking about you a lot actually and what a great wedding that was and just so happy for the both of you and of course spiritual advisor well now I'd be honored because God has a plan for your life and.. -------
.... -------.......
.... -------
.... -------
.... -------
.... -------
.... the line went dead for there was only so much storage space to leave a message of a particular length and he had exceeded the limit.

To make a long story short, yes, Father Lebron reiterated, in a this time, real time, conversation over the phone, come back out to the first date restaurant on the Old Moscow Pullman highway and we'll get right to work. And so, they did. And this time it was not raining but the sky was a deep red and purple as the sun was setting behind lentil hills over a dusty road and it was very aesthetically satisfying and the reunion with Father Lebron, from the bear hugs to the shaking of shoulders back into a hug, was very nice. Father LeBron even pinched Mark's check and smacked him softly across the nose in the Irish hospitality style.

'Before we really get to it,' Father LeBron says, 'here, read this, aloud,' handing Mark a folded-up paper which Mark unfurls quickly. 'To see what I've been up to,' Father Lebron explains, 'it's faster this way and then we can get to what matters.'

In purple ink it reads,

There was an ancient city they called Rome—[22]
a colony of refugees from the ashes of Western Civilization's collapse—
a city, of God, I hope yet still, but far

away from Tiber's mouth: extremely rich
and lazy and entitled they, Americans, had become.   75
When it came to waging war, most fierce,
sadly.   77
I have for many years now set my sights, my aim,
my goal
on reconstructing this land they themselves claim is Heaven's favorite.

A hole in the sky of Cowboy's stadium so God can watch His favorite
team play.
God shed his grace on thee.
America the beautiful,
are you still so? I often
wonder.

Rebuild my Church,   87
He told the wolf whisperer many ages ago.
The least I can do is try,
with all my
might
to do my
part   93
to have God find favor with us,
and sending His blessing
upon us.   96

Even if it has been, us unawares, long years cast across all waters, 97
providentially not fate driven, this land, this people wandering from
sea to seas
of darkness.
It was hard to found Rome.   100
The founding of a Catholic America might prove harder still.

I say the Mass.
I fast.
I pray the Rosary.
I pray the Divine Office.

---

22 Virgil, *The Aeneid* (trans. Mandelbaum), Book I, 1–3.

42

I pray the Divine Mercy Chaplet; not just at 3 PM but all 60 minutes
of the 3 o'clock hour.
I pray the Angelus three times a day; 6, twelve, and 6.
To repair my long strained nerves I
deadlift
and I
dunk.   111

The desert monks of old used to weave baskets and then return to
prayer.
I dunk, and then I deadlift and then I return, myself,
to prayer,
to this spiritual work.

It is hard—this potential City of God, new stars and stripes Rome—I
do and have confessed.
I ask myself, often:

But I—how should I dare? And by whose permission?
I am not Aeneas. Hardly Saint Paul, me.[23]
Who could believe me worthy of even the glimpse, forget the execu-
tion, of this grand
Vision?

But just last week I pulled 605, five
times.
And I dunked, two handed in traffic, three
times
last pick up game with the boys.   127
I've touched eleven foot one in training,
41 inch vertical, confirmed, despite being
59 years old.
100
Percent, I assure you,
God's grace is sufficient unto thee.   133

---

[23] Dante, *The Divine Comedy*, Inferno, Canto II: 32.

'605 5 times,' Mark says. 'So, what's your max?'

'I've loaded 700 on the bar before,' Father LeBron says, 'but no chance, it barely budged. But that's my goal. I think when I pull 700 it will be a sign America is about to become a Catholic nation. My max, though, um, six, six forty, I think.'

'What's a vertical?' Anna asks.

'How high you can jump straight off the ground, straight up,' Mark says.

'Is 41 inches good?' she asks.

Before Mark can answer, for he had emitted an instantaneous snort and head shake, as in *good, good? It's great, it's basically hearing some guy's net worth is somewhere in the billions and asking if that's a lot of money*—Father LeBron is off and up, no warm up, in the act of demonstration and it's just obvious that, wow, this priest has crazy bounce, IPA micro-brewery level hops.

Father LeBron lands and then says, with a tone of finality.

'Now, my friends, and after all this, let's get down to business. Let's talk about why you came here, let's do spiritual advising. Yes, from my own unworthy hands, but really by the grace of God through the writings of Saint Augustine. By the way, do you know what his vertical and deadlift max were?'

Mark and Anna say nothing.

Father LeBron looks at them.

'No,' Mark says, 'what were they?'

'Oh, I have no idea,' Father LeBron replies. 'I was sincerely asking: "do you know what his vertical and deadlift max were?" I don't know, but I would like to know. Anyways, I encourage you, the two of you, to take notes on the following because henceforth and to the end of this session there will be no more distractions, diversions, nothing; nothing but spiritual helps and signposts. So, you ready?

Mark and Anna nod. Anna has her notepad out, yellow paged, blue lined lawyer pad with a **black Bic pen** already uncapped.

Father LeBron begins.

'Lesson 1—because our last and first meeting, which culminated in your wedding, I'm calling lesson 0.—will be demarcated by alphabetically ordered section breaks and so here we set off with

A.

A. One day, at the conclusion of all this, you will write a book called

Mark and Anna, Models.

Owing to your already well-established public profile, this book will do extraordinarily well and make many fall in love with Saint Augustine, therefore with Christ and His Church, and we will all be very grateful to you.

The chapters of this book will be our lessons. Imagine them in blue ink, a blue more like the sky than sea. Actually, just go for that teal of the City of God you've already seen and touched.'

'In each of these, you will recount to the public the lessons that I imparted to you having had them imparted to me by this great saint. He having it imparted to him by the light of God, the sole true Wisdom in all the universe: Jesus Christ, the Eternal Word of God. It will help a lot of people, your book, and so I thank you both, in advance, for writing it.'

B. 'Tonight's session is that future chapter two, the Problem of Evil.

First, definitions.

B.1 Evil does not have a positive nature.

B.2. Evil is lack, privation, deprivation, the absence of a good that should be there but is not.

B.3 Evil therefore is not something, in and of itself, but something missing.

As such the previous session should read like this, with the final word not there.

"Evil therefore is not something, in and of itself, but something   ."

Imagine evil as a corroding agent that, if present, and not scrubbed away by good, holy good, the sole source being God's grace, delivered through the sacraments, it eats away and makes nothing, makes absent, the good that should be there in all its essential goodness. Let's imagine that previous sentence in evil-corroded reduction. It would work, on down, like this:

—Evil therefore is not something, in and of itself, but something missing.

—Evil therefore is not something, in and of itself, but something   .

—Evil therefore is not something, in and of itself, but   .

—Evil therefore is not something, in and   .

—Evil therefore is not   .

—Evil   .

—(24   )

But so then turning to God and asking His forgiveness, and receiving the grace from the Sacrament of Confession, makes a full restitution not just back to a., but a new b.

a. —Evil therefore is not something, in and of itself, but something missing.

b. —Goodness is the original plan. It is integrity and health, in and of itself.

---

24 Can you imagine and frame the contours of pure absence, total void?

B.4. Evil, defect, can only be talked about in reference to the good. God, all good, made all things good. There is only a first, foundational source of good: God, and all God made, again, is good. This Great Good made all goods, plural. There is no original great Bad making small bads. For, back to B.1 through B.3, evil does not have a positive nature or source, it is only the corruption, the rot, the lack of the original good. Reinforcing this,

B.5. Good can exist without evil but not the other way around. Without sin, which is the source of evil, our own corrupted wills willing defect, all things would be wholly good, as they should have been, as is their natural state. All things good, all things integrally operating as they were meant to. But evil can only come into existence off of the good, in response to the good, in corruption of the good. The worst evil, most bad bad, Hell, is this to the maximum: full evil because a complete corruption of good, a complete lacking of the good, and so what results is

utter and perpetual darkness.

Ok, but so,

    C.

        C is the definition of evil straight from the horse's mouth. How does St. Augustine himself define evil in his magisterial *City of God?* I've read this book cover to cover 58 times, and had it memorized after the 27th read, so I will provide the definition and page citation. P.s.,' Father Lebron says, pulling out the book and throwing it at Mark, who catches it against his chest, 'it's yours. My personal, annotated copy. As you can see: the slightly abridged, introduction by Etienne Gilson, 1958 Image/Doubleday Edition, 551 pages into the Index, absolutely ridiculously pretty seafoam green cover with that nice, very yellow sun too. That's what I'll be citing from.

        —p. 217, Book XI, chapter nine, Saint Augustine, quote: "Evil has no positive nature; what we call evil is merely the lack of something that is good." [25]

        One more definition, for good measure, here from —Book XIV, chapter 11, p. 305, St Augustine quote, 'evil cannot exist without good, since the natures to which the defects belong, in as much as they are natures, are good.'[26]

---

[25] St. Augustine, *The City of God* (New York: Image/Doubleday, 1958), 217.
[26] Ibid, 305.

Please note as I progress to state examples that it is all, I mean the overarching umbrella here, about that definition of the City of God that St Augustine provides, right there on page 321, at the end of book fourteen, chapter 28. That the City of God is about the love of God even to the contempt of self, whereas the fallen City of Man is about the love of self even to the contempt of God.[27] Do remember what Mother Angelica of Irondale was wont to say: the only true tragedy in life is sin, the only real evil is sin.

For D and E, I'm going to give you examples. First, D., the general ones one can call small scale evils, lesser lacks, while under the E heading the more serious evils. I'll conclude with a section F on

---

[27] Ibid., 321.

so what does it all mean then; why is there evil; why
does God permit evil?

D. General lacks
  1. In ability to learn music/as in or, learn stuff, period.
  2. Physical, as in sports or sporting, fails.
  3. Small cough, common cold, breakdown of the body.
  4. Lacks in etiquette and interpersonal behavior.
  5. On beauty.

Okay,
so,
D1.

Look at how much small evil, lesser lacks, people suffer in terms of learning. God intended that we know things, Augustine himself writes that we love to know, and know that we love to know things, and, prior to the Fall, it should have been so. Learning should have been effortless; music, languages, calculus, whatever. And for some, praise God, it is. These people are closer to the integral whole of how it should have been, to the good of learning as we are made to experience it. But when you see how some people can't even learn a singular phrase in a language they've been working at for years or claim to be able to play the violin but then you hear them and whatever those sounds are it's certainly not the violin or when you just look around and see the vast seas of ignorance lapping up about us—as it says in the 22nd chapter of the Book of Sirach, quote: teaching a fool is like gluing a broken pot, or rousing another from deep sleep. Whoever talks to a fool talks to someone who is asleep; when it is over he says, "what was that?"[28]—then you see the reality of the missing ingredients of what should be there in terms of learning but is not; is missing; is this lack that signifies evil, even here in a small sense.

D.2.

Physical, as in sports or sporting, fails. Sports are a great explainer of the problem of evil. Sports show, with no room for doubt, how much people lack in abilities that could be there but are not. It is certainly a lack, an evil, no matter how insignificant it may be in the grand scheme of things, to not be able to bench press the bar, to possess a single digit vertical jump, to not be able to run a mile under ten minutes, to not be able to execute even one proper pull

---

[28] Sirach 22:7-8.

up, and so on. Watch sports and you will see much evil, a lot missing that should be there, much missing from the ideal and good wholeness of the matter.

D.3.

Small cough, common cold, breakdown of body and D.4.

Lacks in etiquette and interpersonal behavior are more of the same.

Yes, and thank God, we are still here in this section D of lesser evils, that cold that kept you bedridden for two nights and now that you've recovered from, right, yes, it was not a big deal, but it was an evil, nonetheless, a lack of health, however small and temporary. You should have been out walking the dog, eating mint chocolate chip outside on cobblestone streets while you people watched and laughed and waited for the sun to set so as to take in the stars. But you were, even momentarily, suffering a lack, a deprivation of the physical health that would enable you to be as you were, and are, meant to be. And what to say,

D.4,

of people who burp at the dinner table, who tell explicit jokes to grandmothers, who hug people they just met five minutes ago, who, here being kids, think they can call their friends' parents by their first name, or, worse still, parents who tell their kids' friends to call them by their first names? Certainly, we can say they are engaging in evil, however small of an evil it is, but still, yes, indeed a deprivation, a lack of etiquette and interpersonal behavior understandings.'

Father LeBron pauses to take a drink of water.
He gulps it down with frightful rapidity.
He scrunches the bottle in his hands until it's crushed
and then
he throws it, carelessly,
behind him.
He then falls back in his chair and emits a loud,
'ahhhhhhh, nothing like 2 parts hydrogen and one part
oxygen to wet the whistle. See,'

he then says, following a brief pause.

'That was evil, the
whole thing I just did there. The aggressive public water
gulping, the frat boy inspired littering in disposal of the
bottle, the calling water 2 parts hydrogen . . . well, you see,
um, yes, huge, huge lacks in D.4. etiquette and interpersonal behavior.'

He clears his throat.
Anna and Mark smile.
Father LeBron,

they're both thinking,

well, he demonstrated that, in real time, really well.

That was cool.

Anna, she has not stopped taking the most elegant, calligraphous, and thorough notes. Mark has basically been looking at and thinking about Anna the whole time. He's probably heard anywhere from 17 to 31%[29] of what Father LeBron has said so far.

'D.5.

on Beauty,' Father LeBron says. 'The two of you are about as close to no evil at all when it comes to beauty. I don't mean to embarrass you, either of you, but facts are facts. The two of you being just about as good looking as two people can be, that was supposed to be the norm. Absent the fall, a perfect physical beauty, as you have it, would mirror, would spring forth from, a more important and higher spiritual beauty. You don't think Adam and Eve were physically perfect as much as spiritually so, before the apple, before the banishment following their disobedience? It's supposed to go hand in hand, beauty of the body and beauty of the soul, and

---

[29] Bolded on a 100 scale for reference: 1 2 3 4 5 6 7 8 9 10 11 12 13 14 15 16 **17 18 19 20 21 22 23 24 25 26 27 28 29 30 31** 32 33 34 35 36 37 38 39 40 41 42 43 44 45 46 47 48 49 50 51 52 53 54 55 56 57 58 59 60 61 62 63 64 65 66 67 68 69 70 71 72 73 74 75 76 77 78 79 80 81 82 83 84 85 86 87 88 89 90 91 92 93 94 95 96 97 98 99 100.

yet look around, look and see so much of the defects and lacks and deprivations of beauty all around us, especially in the soul, and that's worst of all.

But, so, having talked about the D. level lower evils, let's discuss five more serious evils.

E. The serious stuff.

    1. Lack of familial love

    2. Lack of charity towards the poor

    3. Physical ailments (here a bigger breakdown than above in D.3)

    4. Crimes, large and small

    5. Wars

E.1

Lack of familial love, what more can one say, for example, about the serious evil of doing so much humanitarian work, and so much public good besides, while your own flesh and blood, your brother, sleeps under a bridge in a bad part of town? Charity starts at home. What does it matter how nice and kind you are to strangers when you not only don't speak to your sister, but wish her all kinds of bad things, even taking perverse pleasure from her struggles and sufferings? This is evil.

And,

E.2,

what does it matter, anything, "good' you might be doing if you not only despise the poor, and look down on them, but ignore them all together? For I was hungry and you gave me not to eat; I was thirsty, and you gave me not to drink...

The small cough and short illness lacks, the evil of that we discussed above in D.3 is all the more acutely felt in

E.3

serious ailments, lifelong chronic conditions, terminal illnesses, even just with the advancing old age inabilities to complete the menial items once so easily done. Christ Himself told St Peter,

But when thou shalt be old, thou shalt stretch forth thy hands, and another shall
     gird thee, and lead thee whither thou wouldst not.[30]

---

[30] John 21:18.

Anyone experiencing a serious illness can tell you much, from first-hand experience, about the nature of evil, about things lacking, deprivations, a missing health most noticed the moment it has departed.

'Rest assured,' Father LeBron says, now drinking a beer, the golden color of it properly resplendent, 'rest assured that D.4 and D.5. crimes, large and small, but especially, the former, the sordid and sensational and "oh, that, now that is evil" type crimes and the wars that plague the global like a plague of locusts, rest assured they too, in their evilness, spring from this same deprivation and lack; a lack of love of neighbor, absolutely, and obviously, but a lack for that first part of the two greatest commandments[31] most especially.

---

[31] Matthew 22:36-40: 'Teacher, which is the greatest commandment in the Law?' Jesus replied: 'Love the Lord your God with all your heart and with all your soul and with all your mind. This is the first and greatest commandment. And the second is like it: Love your neighbor as yourself. All the Law and the Prophets hang on these two commandments.'

For it is above all hatred for God, the lack
of love of God and His divinely willed order,
that leads men into the deprived darkness
of crime and war. Rather, into all sin.

So,' Father LeBron says before pausing. 'Did you,' to Mark, 'did you get that, all that?'

'What?' Mark says.

'That,' Father LeBron says, 'The...you were, you weren't paying attention, right?

'Uh...—

'You were just thinking about Anna the whole time.'

'Yeah,' Mark admits.

Father LeBron exhales through the nose and then bites his lip.

'You were just zoning out, thinking about Anna, the whole time, instead of listening to what I'm trying to teach you.'

'Yeah,' Mark says, 'Yep.'

It's about to get testy between these two men until...Anna to the rescue. She shows Father LeBron her notebook. She's taken four, count'em, one, two, three, four pages of notes. She's written down everything he has said, hasn't missed a point, even circled and underlined a few items.

Father LeBron smiles. Then he says,

'Ok, so, guys, my friends, look, this then brings us to
F.

Why is there evil?
Why does God allow evil?
What is the point,

anyways?

First, I think we have to understand, and *rejoice, in the
fact that we are not God* and whereas He is not bound by
time and space but the possessor of an eternal, unchanging vision, we are, and so we don't know how it all fits
together and maybe even some things we think are bad
are not in fact bad but we just don't see how it all fits
together and all we can do, as men and women of faith,
is trust God. Live that Divine Mercy image motto,

"Jesus, I trust in You"

and that fruit of the first sorrowful mystery, the Agony
in the Garden,

resignation to God's will.

God has a plan, for you personally, and *the* plan, in general, too. The victory has already been won, but we have to do our part and say yes to Him and trust in Him. Remember,

.....we know that all things work together for good for those who love God, who are called according to his purpose.[32]

But if you want even a little more than that, in conclusion,' Father LeBron says, 'I'd say that God ultimately allows evil only to bring about a greater good. In the book of Genesis, Joseph, he never becomes Egyptian Grain Czar and Prime Minister without first being thrown in a cistern by his moron brothers. Their evil brought about a greater good and Joseph even says this, it's right there in Genesis, that the evil they wished to do to him has been turned by God into good.[33] God ultimately allows evil only to bring about a greater good. And it's tied up in our free will. We have free will. Listen to what St Augustine says about that: "God is the Cause of all causes, although not of all choices" and "man's will is all important. If it is badly directed, the emotions will be perverse; if it is rightly directed, the emotions will be not merely blameless but praiseworthy."[34]

Therefore, because we have free will, we can say no and we did, Adam and Eve did. That's the origin of evil, the original deprivation, choosing
                not God,
            choosing a defective destiny
                apart from God.

---

[32] Romans 8:28.
[33] Genesis 50:20.
[34] St. Augustine, *The City of God* (1958 ed) Book V, ch. 8, 103 and Book XIV, ch. 6, 303.

But from that evil, what comes? A greater good. The Incarnation, the Word Made flesh and dwelling among us, the God-Man, perfectly innocent, suffering the apparent greatest evil in human history, Deicide, God crucified by his sinful and rebellious creation, but all this only to bring about the greatest good: Easter Sunday, Eternal Glory, for, amen, amen again:

dying YOU destroyed our death, rising YOU restored our life. Saint Augustine said,

FELIX CULPA, and he was right.

He was absolutely right.'

With that the first session was over, yeah, that was it, that was all.
Anna and Mark thanked the good priest profusely, maybe they even over did it.
Ah, no worries.
The three friends talked long into the night. They had a sumptuous dinner and then three rounds of dessert and Mark and Father LeBron drank beers and Anna brought out a really nice bottle of wine, from where, no one knew, and it was very, **very dark outside, here,** somewhere on the Old Moscow Pullman Highway.

It was late.

But then Father LeBron challenged Mark to a game of basketball, one on one, and Mark was incredibly impressed seeing Father Lebron's 41 inch vertical slowly being revved up as they warmed up and it seemed like he, Father LeBron, could dunk on command and any which way and man, what athleticism.

Mark won the game 21-0, 2s and 3s make it, take it. 21-0 because while Father LeBron had that insane bounce and was super strong, his world class deadlift giving him a sturdy foundation in the paint, he almost literally couldn't dribble, like it looked like he didn't know what dribbling a basketball meant, like he had never done it before, and the six shots that he got off—remember, make it, take it, and Mark had been a reserve guard in high school who's one outstanding skill was three point shooting—were all air balls, one missing the hoop by at least 20 feet, wide right, and Mark, as it was happening was actually really embarrassed by that, embarrassed for Father LeBron, by how bad the priest was at actually playing the game. I mean, he, he just legit sucked at basketball.

Anna and Mark thanked Father Lebron a final time.
They left.

The not luckless Anna, poor luckless Dido,[35]   134
had drawn out the night with varied talk. She now drank
long love and asked her Aeneas many questions:
about his Dad, about this other dude who was a certified chad,
how a woman's son
was armed, I mean this guy, Mark's cousin, he was like too jacked,
right? Please stop
doing bicep curls, my friend.   140
And now, how exactly strong were the guys Mark
lifted with; I mean, the don't skip leg day, correct?; But how tremen-
dous was her Achilles,

he, Mark, and at that Mark smiled through deep self-satisfaction at
such lofty
comparisons so carelessly   144
put out: into the air, the open, the long cold, see freezing
nighttime air.

'My love,' Anna calls, 'tell me all things
from the first beginning: what is swagger(?),
what did your family think of you becoming a model, and then your
journeyings
right up to the very moment you laid eyes on her,
I mean me. For now the seventh summer carries us,
poor pilgrims in this vale of tears, across the Old Moscow Pullman
Highway
and waters.'   153

---

[35] Virgil, *The Aeneid* (trans. Mandelbaum), Book I, 26–27.

3

Attractions and Attachments

'Babe, c'mon,' Anna says, pulling out her phone to check the time. She starts tapping on the screen nervously. 'Our plane leaves in less than three hours. You remember what happened with my mom's flight to Atlanta last year.'

'Yep,' Mark says, nodding but not taking his eyes off the screen. His fingers move about the controller with the effortlessness of a man deep in familiar territory. It's probably this way for pianists, car mechanics, plumbers. Can do it blindfolded, second nature. Mark is, and has been, playing *NCAA football 2002*, an old college football video game, on the verifiably ancient PlayStation 2 console, for a while this afternoon.

How long?

Impossible to say. He honestly wouldn't even be able to guess. He had had breakfast, two bowls of *Cinnamon Toast Crunch*[36], and was now on a third cup of coffee, milk[37] foamed twice over each time, lots of squirts of the bear bottle honey,[38] sipping every now and then but otherwise staring at the screen playing, playing, no, working, yes, perfecting his craft as the minutes passed into hours the hours themselves bundled together.

'Babe,' Anna says, still standing there in the doorway. Man, she looked good, Mark thought. Not that he was going to be taken away from the work, even by her, but

---

[36] Nutrition facts (abridged version): serving size 1 cup (41g). Calories 170/Total Fat 4g/Total Carbohydrate 33g/Dietary Fiber 3 g/Total Sugars 12 g/Protein 2g/Vitamin D 4mcg/Calcium 130mg/iron 3.6 mg.

[37] From a cow. One cup of the whole variant clocking in at 7.86 grams of protein and 0.26 mg of niacin.

[38] 11mg potassium, 17g sugars, 0.1g protein per 1, 64 calorie tablespoon (21g) serving; from bees, ideally, dare we dream, from an apiary in Iowa.

each time he laid eyes on her his dominant emotion was gratitude. She was so terribly, ridiculously, even pathetically good looking.

'Babe,' she says, again, now with noticeable impatience, almost whining. 'I mean it. I'm serious. We should have left fifteen minutes ago. You know how traffic can be. My mom had to be rerouted though, through like Pensacola or something. Like, ewww. All because she showed up late. C'mon, let's leave.'

Mark exhales. 'Okay, okay, baby, okay,' still focused on the work, hands operating the controller like a mechanic closing the hood on his 42,885th successful oil change. All that's left to do is ask the customer if he wants a receipt and affix that sticker on the inside of the windshield. Anna simply does not understand. There are less than two minutes left in the game and it's the final game of the season before the bowls start. He can't just turn off the console, all his progress will be lost. Mark's virtual Idaho Vandals are 11-0, about to be 12-0, and ranked number one in the nation. A trip to the Rose Bowl, for the National Championship, is all but assured. But he has to finish this game first.

It's

Vandals 105, Fresno State 7,
1:52 left to go in the fourth quarter.

Mark's Create a player super team—his 6'10, 360 lb QB, Hebe OneofthemOnes, first name Hebe[39], last name OneofthemOnes, and his star 7'1, 400 lb but 4.2 speed WR, first name TheyGonBe, last name SoCooked—have teamed up, just in this game, for 702 yards and thirteen touchdowns[40] through the air.

'I'm serious,' Anna says, now all but pleading. 'Please. Let's go. Please.'

'Okay,' Mark says, 'okay. You're right. Just...,' frantically, in an inward, internal sense, scanning his options to run out the necessary time and save the game but also appease his wife who is actually in the right and wants him to just unplug the stupid game, now, and leave, now, because they should have left long ago.

'I need to go to the bathroom. Two minutes, I'll hurry.'

'I'll wait for you outside,' she says.

Mark makes a start for the bathroom. Waits........
.... hears Anna exit the house.

Returns to the console.

Tries kneeling the ball but stupid Fresno State calls a timeout both times. It's 105-7, you idiots! Stop stalling. Don't you know how angry my wife is going to be? Ah, you morons! And so, on third down Mark does the most sensible thing he can think of to finally end the game. He puts Hebe OneofthemOnes into shotgun formation, 5 WR, all go routes, and upon receiving the snap makes him sprint backwards towards

↓

↓

↓

---

[39] Pronounced 'He be;' as in, 'he is,' as in 'he is OneofthemOnes*'
* one of those very special, unique players.
[40] That's exceptionally good.

↓

↓

↓

↓ his own goal line.

There, he pauses

. . . . .   then back down
                                            ↑ the other sideline ↓

. . . . .   ↑   ↓

                                    up the
. . . . .   ↑ sideline, ↑   ↓

. . . . .   ↑   ↓

. . . . .   ↑   ↓

. . . . .   ↑   ↓

. . . . . then up the field, ↑   ↓

                                                        ↓

                                                        ↓

                                                        ↓

                                            ↓

                                            ↓

                                            ↓

                                            ↓

                                            ↓

                                            ↓

                            until the clock hits

0:00

This could, hypothetically and theoretically, go on all day. Mark is playing on the easiest setting, fatigue is turned off, and OneofthemOnes, just like SoCooked, has 4.2, if not even 4.1 or four flat speed so...it could go on like this for a long time.

But because Fresno State had the temerity to call time-outs, twice, when all Mark wanted to do was end the game like a gentleman, he has his quarterback take off from the five-yard line, showboating in midair, as he clips the pylon with an outstretched arm, football extended, on a final dive into the end zone.

Idaho Vandals 111
Fresno State Bulldogs 7

Mark saves the game.
Mark joins Anna
outside.
Mark
and Anna

leave

for the airport.

They made it on time, failing that but five minutes late. What ensued next is so ridiculous, so stupid, so dumb and seemingly made-up, absolutely did not happen except for the fact that

it did,

no way, no way that actually happened, no, wait, what(?), really(?),

yes,

it really did,

you're telling me, no, c'mon, there is no, I mean,

stop,

stop,

stop,

stop,

there is no way, not in a million years but ... wait,

it did though,
it really did happen

so much like that, all that, that one can just pass by
without comment and pick up the story after their flights
back to Father Lebron were successfully completed and
they found themselves on the Old Moscow Pullman
Highway

yet again.

Wait,
okay, wait,
okay,

okay, okay, okay, okay, okay, okay, okay, okay, okay, okay,
okay, okay, okay, okay, okay, okay, okay, okay, okay, okay,
okay, okay, okay, okay, okay, okay, okay, okay, okay, okay,
okay, okay, okay, okay, okay, okay, okay, okay, okay, okay,
okay, okay, okay, okay, okay, okay, okay, okay, okay, okay,
okay, okay, okay, okay, okay, okay, okay, okay, okay, okay,
okay, okay, okay, okay, okay, okay, okay, okay, okay, okay,
okay, okay, okay, okay, okay, okay, okay, okay, okay, okay,
okay, okay, okay, okay, okay, okay, okay, okay, okay, okay,
okay, okay, okay, okay, okay, okay, okay, okay, okay, okay,
okay, okay, okay, okay, okay, okay, okay, okay, okay, okay,
okay, okay, okay, okay, okay, okay, okay, okay, okay, okay,
okay, okay, okay, okay, okay, okay, okay, okay, okay, okay,
okay, okay, okay, okay, okay, okay, okay, okay, okay, okay,
okay, okay, okay, okay, okay, okay, okay, okay, okay, okay,
okay, okay, okay, okay, okay, okay, okay, okay, okay, okay,
okay, okay, okay, okay, okay, okay, okay, okay, okay, okay,
okay, okay, okay, okay, okay, okay, okay, okay, okay, okay,
okay, okay, okay, okay, okay, okay, okay, okay, okay, okay,
okay, okay, okay,

Let it be told. But only the facts; and as brief as can be.

Mark and Anna arrived at the airport but, due to the chaos of feeling like they were going to be late, forgot to use the special side entrance. Panic ensued.

41

was the kind of catch all, general response, as crowds flocked around them, trying to get a picture, even just a glance.

The ever growing but still manageable crowd quickly swelled to unmanageable proportions. Gates 35-39[42] in Concourse B, which were supposed to be taking people to Cincinnati, San Antonio, Phoenix, Dallas, and Seattle, respectively, emptied *en masse* as a mass of people began to clog the doorway near where Mark and Anna had first been spotted. Gate attendants, too, they wanted to see the stars and once the pilots themselves made their way back down the jetway, and into the crowd, a full-blown crisis was on hand.

Problems begat problems as more and more people pushed closer and more and more kept fainting—the

Heyburn Front Desk Effect,

as the phenomenon was being called—from the sight of Mark and Anna's truly dangerous beauty. Luckily, Mark was always good at thinking on his feet. He dumped out the contents of two recently purchased bags from the newspaper shop but a few steps away—two magazines, 3 bags of skittles, 2 packs of bubble gum, and a Snickers bar,

---

[41] 'Look, wow, no way, look, it's Mark and Anna!'

[42] Concourse B
Comprehensive Gate Listings
1, 2, 3, 4, 5, 6, 7, 8, 9, 10, 11, 12, 13, 14, 15,
16, 17, 18, 19, 20, 21, 22, 23, 24, 25, 26, 27, 28, 29, 30
31, 32, 33, 34, **35, 36, 37, 38, 39**, 40, 41, 42, 43, 44, 45,
46, 47, 48, 49

Mark and Anna always shared a Snickers when traveling together—and put one bag over Anna's head, the other over his.

The storm broke.
People stopped fainting.
The crowd staggered

out of its stupor and regained something like a general bearing. Too late for Cincinnati, that flight was supposed to have departed 45 minutes ago. Seattle too. Needless to say, the offending pilots, gate, and flight attendants got quite the earful from higher ups in the FAA later on.

. . . . >>>>>>>>>>>>>>>>>

'I don't care if the Easter Bunny walking hand in hand with Santa Claus shows up at the airport, Anderson!,' one of these FAA bigwigs said, no, yelled into the conference call transmitter at one of the pilots, a no nonsense professional of the highest order, John Anderson, a no accidents/no complaints logger of thousands of hours of commercial flight time following a decorated career in the United States Air Force. 'You stay at your post . . . you . . . I can't, I can't believe I have to say this! I can't believe I am reprimanding someone like you over . . . over exiting an about to push off airplane to go see some stupid movie stars! This has to be the most asinine "incident" I have ever dealt with in the entirety of my career.'

'She's not a movie star,' Anderson said. 'She's a model.'

' . . . '

'Anna Davenport,' Anderson said.

'Dupont,' another pilot said, correcting him. 'She married Mark Dupont. He's also a model.'

'She's a model,' Anderson said, again. 'Look, you're right, of course. And it won't happen again. But she's... she's her,[43] she's the one, *the* model, okay?'

The FAA CEO or HR or whatever guy on the other end of the line said nothing. Soon, the line went dead.

The only silver lining was the steady hum-buzz static that followed disconnection, a warm sound that when held steady could wash over a person from head to toe, washing away stress, tension, and all the cares in the world too.

<<<<<<<<<<<<<<<<<<<<<<<<<. . . . .

Anna and Mark board the plane.

To avoid a repeat of the pre-boarding process they get to sit up front, in the cockpit with the pilots. These are serious men, Air Force trained, combat tested, and can handle the sheer shock factor of Mark and Anna's good looks. There will not be any fainting up here.

A little over an hour into the flight Mark turns to ask Anna a question. She ignores him. He keeps trying to get her attention, but she's locked into a screen, the pale glow of the blue light lighting up her face, her eyes darting across the screen time and again. Mark tries a final time, nudging his wife on the shoulder.

'Hey,' she says, 'what? What is it?'

'I wanna tell you something,' Mark says.

'What?' but now looking away from him, again, eyes on the screen.

'Ah, I see,' Mark says, laughing, 'so when I'm playing some stupid, dumb video game it's like, baby, stop, baby let's go. We have to leave. But then here's you, sucked into Pinterest like you always get. It's okay when you do it, got it.'

---

[43] SheBe OneofthemOnes.

'This is different,' Anna says, still scrolling.

'How?'

'Because we're not late for a plane. That's how.'

Mark laughs. 'Okay, whatever you need to tell yourself.'

Now Anna laughs and closes the screen. 'What did you wanna tell me?"

'I wrote a rap song about you,' Mark says. 'I've been working on it the whole time, the whole flight. Do you wanna hear it?'

Anna says nothing. But she keeps looking at him and so Mark dives into the first few verses.

One shoulder shimmy, from Anna, then a second, that's all Mark needed to see. That was all the feedback validation he needed. She was loving it, okay, alright, let's get it then.

And so he did.

Mark launched into the full lyrics with gusto. Anna stood up, right there in the cockpit, and started dancing, full on. The thing about Anna nee Davenport now Dupont forever and ever more, is that she is not just a great model. The best, yes, hands down. But a good cook, speaks perfect French and Spanish too? Yep, and look, this girl can really, really dance. Anna can do the two things most important in dancing: execute the moves with fluidity, but, also, and just as important, in rhythm with the music that is serving as background and foundational base. Anna is dancing in perfect rhythm to Mark's rapping and Mark, seeing how much his wife is loving it, is getting more into it with each and every line.

The lead pilot is the one and same John Anderson. He's unaffected. Eyes ahead, focused on doing his job and nothing else. Sincere in his intention that he'll never have another lapse of judgment on the job ever again. So, he's good. But the co-pilot, he's been locked in since Anna first stood up. He's been hype-manning Mark with 'yeah,' 'uh-huh,' 'yet,' 'uh-huh,' 'okay, yet' and stuff like that. It's actually working really well from a musical, auditory reception perspective. Then, despite this being a night flight, he puts on sunglasses, lowrides his pilot cap over those sunglassed eyes, and starts dancing, while still seated, in the fashion of hands crossed at the wrist rotating back and forth out front, extended.

The flight lands safely not much later on. The connector goes ahead with precisely zero drama; in boarding, in-flight, all. Anna sleeps through the whole second flight. Sometime there-during Mark puts a blanket over her to keep her warm and kisses her on top of the head and then himself drifts................ off to........................
....
....
.
.
....
...
....
....

sleep.

They wake by way of bright lights overhead directly to the face, the eyes, the, what time is it? Rental car waiting, they push the button, make those turns and, before they know it, they find themselves crunching along the most beautiful dirt road in these Unites States—the Old Moscow Pullman Highway—on their way to the secret restaurant where not long after their first date they were married, on their way to see their spiritual advisor, the one and only, by God's grace good, Father LeBron.

The power of America would by God's sovereign grace[44]   154
never be overturned, like proud Ilium, fallen,
and all of Caesar's once grand Rome smoking from the ground,
this the Highest One, in His Providence, was pleased to allow.
See we, Mark and Anna, driven by divine commands
and signs to sail in search of fields of exile   160
yes, behold, these endless lentil hills, this well milled gravel, the high blue skies,
have made once distant and deserted lands familiar.
The Old Moscow Pullman Highway, a second home second
to none, as by terms of beauty we judge and frame and hold on to,
even when only by memories are our access points permitted. We aim to build
a fleet of theological arguments and helps. This book, that Father Lebron
has assured us one day will see the light
of day in the lentil hills
of the fertile Palouse. Knowing not where God's providence
will carry us or where we are to settle;   170
and there we gather up our men; maybe other models,
like us. Maybe not
like us. Time and God's time will
tell.
No sooner was summer come upon us when my father
and Anna's mother bid us spread our sails to the falsely called fate
that is, in truth,
God's will.   177
Anna, weeping, declared she must forever give up the shores and harbors
of Mobile Bay, of South Alabama up into the rivers and hamlets of
her very own
Kingdom of Tennessee where thrice the crown was placed, reverently,
upon her head,
even in absentia.
Mark, he too declared that Concordia, Kansas, that which was my home,
those Great Plains of corn and sunsets and tornadoes and summer-
time hail,
I bid thee farewell as long as God might require.
And they had done that: the sweet bonds of Holy Matrimony, a new life,
together.

---

[44] Virgil, *The Aeneid* (trans. Mandelbaum), Book III, 55.

Approaching the secret restaurant yet again, Mark and Anna couldn't help feeling that

as exiles banished somewhere east of Eden we go out across the waters.
Yet together, as best friends, as man and wife, as models.

Out across waters of doubt and faith but ever assured that trusting in Him, 190

God, 191

we will have entrusted well. 192

'What's up, homies?' Father Lebron says, walking up to Mark and Anna and giving them each a hug. 'How was your trip?'

'Good,' Mark says. 'How are you?'

'Excellent. Come on in. I'm on my last set. I'll hit that, we can eat, then get down to business.

'It's quarter past midnight,' Mark says.

'Yeah,' Fr. Lebron says. 'I do my best lifting after 10 pm. Don't know why, but it is what it is. Have been deadlifting for almost two hours now. Come here, check this out.'

They follow Fr. LeBron to his makeshift gym behind the restaurant. It is a Bulgarian Method Eastern European Olympic lifter's architectural dream. Think Rocky, think Drago, think Arnold from the 1977 documentary *Pumping Iron*. Think excellent class level A+ bar and bumper plates and a fantastic lifting floor platform but think, also, you're outside, the smell and sight of the Old Moscow Pullman highway, think the moon and moonlight, think about dreams dreamt, think goals and goals fulfilled, and think, maybe most of all, about a lone animal somewhere out there howling, and bugs buzzing, and weights clanking, and random chairs and broken pipes and empty milk cartons and yellow flip pads filled up with blue ink and pale light emanating from a nearly broken, in need of an electrician pronto, source and just one more rep and the payoff afterwards in terms of the food to be eaten; afterwards.

Father LeBron hits 775 pounds for a triple, each rep clean and controlled. What a monster, Mark thinks, what a beast.

The three sit down to a scrumptious dinner. Father LeBron cooked it all in advance and had it waiting, covered, heated, for their arrival. London broil; potatoes and carrots; cubed and mashed; cooked asparagus and almonds to sprinkle on top; Idaho Huckleberries like you can buy roadside all throughout Idaho, they ate the huckleberries with zero decorum, like animals, hand to mouth, hand to mouth, again and again; French Onion soup, beforehand; and for dessert, well, Anna, she brought dessert, and it's a dessert that cannot really be described or categorized, by categorized what is meant is genre-ified, but they eat it, they ate all of it, everything of everything, and drank a few mugs, the foam falling over the edges of the mugs, mugs of beer. And some coffee with the dessert, too. They eventually looked at a digital, tableside clock and saw it was

2:11 A.M.

Fr LeBron opined that perhaps they should all get some sleep and do the spiritual advising thing first thing in the morning but Anna said she was not tired and Mark said that he was not tired and Father LeBron laughed and said 'no, me neither,' and so they decided, basically, let's get to it then,
now.

'Today's lesson is Attractions and Attachments,' Father Lebron says. 'Your whole trip here has been a lesson in itself. By the way,' he says, anticipating the next question. 'I can read souls. Some great saints throughout history have been able to. I'm not saying I'm that, far from it. In fact, Lord Jesus Christ, Son of the Living God, have mercy on me a sinner. But, God, for whatever reason, in His providence, has deigned to give me this gift and something like, like,' he starts snapping his fingers look-ing for the right words. 'Something like knowing things outside of my immediate sense perception field of vision, if you will. I saw, if "saw," is the right word, your whole trip and so I want to begin this lesson by analyzing it in light of attractions and attachments.'

'Wait, wait, wait,' Mark says, visibly angry. 'You what? You can, like see what we're up to all the time? Like if I'm having a bad day and I'm stuck in traffic and I start f-bomb, f-bomb, f-bomb, you like see that, hear that?'

'No, you idiot,' Father Lebron says.

Being called an idiot makes Mark laugh out loud.

'No,' Father Lebron continues. 'I'm your spiritual advisor, right? You've asked me to help you, by God's grace, grow closer to God. God allows me to see only that which is needed for the process of helping form you two. You're special. I told you about how good your book is going to do. You're both going to help people a lot, and in the way that matters: getting them closer to God, helping them on the road to Heaven. But you have to complete this training, if you want to call it that. We've talked about the City of God v. the City of Man and the problem of evil. You have those lessons and, Anna, my compliments once more: excellent, excellent note taking.'

Anna smiles and taps her notebook with her pen.

'Today we're discussing Attractions and Attachments,' Father Lebron says. 'So ... can we get to it?'

Mark and Anna nod.

'Your trip: case closed. A perfect study in attractions and attachments. Mark, wow, 8 hours of playing video game college football? Are you serious, are you for real? Cut that in half, and use the other four hours for good and productive stuff, and your four hours playing a video game would still be four hours too much. You want to unwind? Relax? Fine. I'm not saying a video game is worse than smoking a cigar,[45] watching a movie, walking

---

[45] People have smoked for a long time, so long it feels like 'time

a dog, or playing cards. But maybe, just play one game. Let OneofthemOnes find SoCooked deep five, six, seven times. Beat a team 100-0. Then turn it off, break free from this—Anna's not wrong—very stupid attachment. And Anna,' now pointing at her, 'Mark's absolutely right about you and Pinterest, TikTok, YouTube Shorts. 6 hours doomscrolling "what's the best granite countertop?" For granite countertops ten minutes should be sufficient, half an hour if you're a moron. And then look at all those poor people mobbing you at the airport, attracted by your model personas to the point of sycophantic attachment. How many of those people could be better fathers and mothers, husbands and wives, bakers, accountants, and downtime relaxers if they tended

---

immemorial.' Then, recently, within the past 80-100 years smoking became very much 'in,' very cool, conspicuous in the mouths of movie stars, dashing pilots, the whole World War II deal, that 'Greatest Generation' and that carried over into the everyone smokes 1950s and kept on cruising until even more recently—since the 1980s? certainly into the and so dated from the 1990s—it was very much 'out.' Smoking was not only bad for you, very, very bad for you but was the complete opposite in terms of social credit of what it had once been. Before, it made you 10 points cooler, now -10 ten points; a sign of sophistication, before, only total losers do it now. And then the D. A. R. E. programs of the early 2000s and all those warning labels and all the horrible commercials chronicling the effects of prolonged smoking, even secondhand smoke. And then once again—because is 2020 the new 1920?—smoking is kind of in again; cigars, pipes, maybe even cigarettes are getting the 'well, it depends' if not the 'actually, smoking is positively good for you.' Only one thing can be said in response to all of this: can you guys please get it together? Which one is it? If it depends, then it's good. Because if it's good in some circumstances that means for some people it can always be good. A little bit of chocolate and a small serving of ice cream is 'it depends.' So, which one is it? Or is it truly just as bad as they said in 1983 just now we have millennials, and Generation Z, and whoever else thinks everything has to have 'my spin put on this' and 'I heard a podcast' but, in reality, these people should be slapped twice, made to wear a dunce cap, and told to shut up? Or, are they right? Which one is it? You've had more than enough time to figure this out.

the garden of their own business[46] instead of insatiably
seeking the next celebrity sighting? St. John of the Cross
said, and he was right, boy was he ever:

It does not matter if a bird is tied down by a chain or a piece of
thread; either way, it cannot fly.

We must be attracted, ultimately to nothing but God,

---

[46] Not a fan of Voltaire, at all. F. May God have mercy upon him.

we must prefer nothing to God. Robert Cardinal Sarah
wrote a great book getting right to the heart of this
matter:

God or Nothing.

All things that are, that exist, as Saint Augustine so beautifully explained, are good because all God made is good. Evil, as you learned last time, is nothing but the absence of good. All things that are, are good. Video games, properly used, with detachment, are good. Granite countertops and social media, properly used, are good. And how good are those we love; our family, our friends? But meditate on what Christ means when he says unless a man hates his father and mother, he is not worthy of Him. What He means, I dare say, is that unless we love NOTHING before Him—similar to how the first commandment commands us to love nothing and no one before God, God first and God above all—we will not be doing it properly. We will be sinning, ensuring our own misery, falling short of the goal. Conversely, put God first, make God your center and all, seek first the Kingdom of God and then, as the 6th chapter of Saint Matthew's Gospel tells, us, quote, "all else will be added unto you."

That's the whole lesson of Attractions and Attachments, guys. All things that are, are good, because God, who made them, is good. God wants you to enjoy good things but in a good way, with proper detachment. Look at the fruit of the third joyful mystery, the Birth of Our Lord and Savior, Jesus Christ. It is "detachment from the world." Mark, it is amazing, incredible how much you love Anna and how devoted you are to her and she to you. But you both must hate each other in comparison to God. Be detached from all, save for God. Attach, fully, to God. Be attracted to nothing more than God, the source of all attractive things.

GOD

first,

last,

in between.

Now,' Father Lebron pauses to take a drink of water then pulls out a beer, pops the top and chugs it frat boy style in 2.9 seconds tops. He shakes his head again, then to another beer disposed of with similar results. 'Now, let's conclude by hearing some quotes from the man himself, Augustine, the spiritual advisor of your spiritual advisor, if you will, all of us taught by the one sole source of Wisdom Himself, for He is WISDOM HIMSELF, Jesus Christ.

Some quotes[47] from Augustine about the nature of attachments, varied attachments, and maybe even how to overcome them. I'll quote them as they are, apart from any of my analysis, the sole exception being the first one. It's about resentment, clinging to resentment. So, when you hear it add, if you'd like, "attachment to," here resentment and, likewise, throughout.'

---

[47] St. Augustine, *The City of God* (1958 ed) Book XV, chpt 22; McShaunessaey, *The Interconnected Web-Currents of Saint Augustine of Hippo's Thought*, 341–422.

1. Resentment is like drinking poison and waiting for the other person to die.

2. This is the very perfection of a man, to find out his own imperfections.

3. Beauty is indeed a good gift of God; but that the good may not think it a great good, God dispenses it even to the wicked.

4. The desire for fame tempts even noble minds.

5. As to those feebler spirits who, though they cannot be said to prefer earthly possessions to Christ, do yet cleave to them with a somewhat immoderate attachment, they have discovered by the pain of losing these things how much they were sinning in loving them. For their grief is of their own making.

6. God is always trying to give good things to us, but our hands are too full to receive them.

7. Thus, a good man, though a slave, is free; but a wicked man, though a king, is a slave. For he serves, not one man alone, but what is worse, as many masters as he has vices.

'As he has vices,' Father Lebron repeats, 'or, we can say, as he has attachments. As many masters as he has attachments. So, to truly close, if you're looking for advice from Augustine on how to properly moderate all attachments and attractions I direct you to that teal covered copy of the City of God, pages 436 though 440, chapter 4 of book 19 of The City of God.

To wit,
quote:

"I speak especially of temperance . . . which must bridle our fleshly lusts if they are not to drag our will to consent to abominations of every sort . . . prudence. Is not this virtue constantly on the lookout to distinguish what is good from what is evil, so that there may be no mistake made in seeking the one and avoiding the other? Justice, . . . to see that to each is given what belongs to each . . . fortitude . . . is not its very function—to bear patiently with misfortune—overwhelming evidence that human life is beset with unhappiness, however wise a man may be?"[48]

'End quote, Saint Augustine of Hippo,' Father LeBron says. 'The only way out of this obvious unhappiness, this general depression and deflation, is Jesus Christ, the Way, the Truth, the Life and you,' pointing at Mark and Anna, this time with the hand holding that copy of The City of God, 'are going to help people find that path, find Christ and His Church.'

---

[48] St. Augustine, *The City of God* (1958 ed), Book XIX, chpt 4, 439–440.

Father Lebron stops talking.

He had been standing.

He sits down.

They started this whole spiritual advising session past 2 am and now the sun is slowly coming up on the Old Moscow Pullman highway.

Not as clear nor as nice as it could slash would be because it is raining, and has been raining,

hard.

'I wonder what the drive back to the airport's going to be like,' Anna says. 'Like, if the road's going to be too soupy, mushy, that kind of thing.'

'Oh, it'll be mushy alright,' Father Lebron says. 'But, guys, you're not going anywhere. Not for a little while anyways.'

Mark exhales. 'We have a connector to Seattle this afternoon. Then another one before the final leg home.'

'Nah,' Father LeBron says.

Mark exhales again, this time drawing it out longer, then snaps his fingers and says, 'You know, don't you? This is that, I can read, I can see, that thing, right?'

Father Lebron smiles and opens a little cream packet into his just made coffee. There really is nothing like the smell of coffee early in the morning.

'Yep.'

'Father,' Anna says, clutching her notebook to her chest. 'You mean, we, we're staying here, with you?'

'Yep....

Would either of you like a cup of coffee.... no? Okay, it's very good. It's hazelnut mocha

. . . .

..... okay, fine, suit yourself.'

'For how long?' Anna asks.

'Oh, now, not that long. Not really that long at all but—

'But you know,' Mark says, stepping forward. 'You

actually know how long, like how many days, or how many hours, how many...-

'Yep.'

'So how long?'

'Nah.'

'You're really not going to tell us?'

'Nope.'

'Why?'

'Don't feel like it... look,' Father Lebron now pours a second cream packet in. 'Don't worry about it. I told you: God has a plan. Look outside. It's going to rain cats and dogs, dogs and cats, elephants and pterodactyls,

-dactyls

-dactyls

-dactyls

-dactyls

Ta, Ta, Ta Ta,

Ta,

Ta-terrrrrrra,

-dactyls. So,

you're not going anywhere. Then, all this rainfall is going to

freeze,

freeze,

freeze,

freeze,

freeze,

The Old Moscow Pullman Highway is going to experience a mini, brief Ice Age. Four horsemen are going to show up. We'll talk. We still have chastity, proto-Protestantism, and Time—especially the Eternal Now—to discuss. Then, *it* will happen. And *it* is going to be awesome. You're going to dominate and, for the final time, by God's grace, help a lot of people grow closer to God.'

'Just tell me: is this the End Times or not?' Mark says.

'Why do you have to go full dumbass?' Father Lebron says. 'No, no.'

'Full dumbass,' Mark counters, 'Full dumbass? Me? You're a priest whose name is LeBron. You look 95 years old but you have the athleticism of a 20-something Olympic athlete. You can also read minds. You're telling us we have to stay here and there's going to be an ice age and that four horsemen are going to show up. Four horsemen! I'm going full dumbass? That's literally in the Book of Revelation, that phrase, the four horsemen of the apocalypse.'

Father LeBron takes a sip of his coffee. 'You're right. No, you're right. I apologize. I totally see your point. Still, no, not the End Times. Not that. But it's going to be cool. And all I'll say is, well, stay tuned.'

Father LeBron hands Mark a cup of hazelnut mocha.

'Dang, this is good,' Mark says.

'I know,' Father LeBron says. 'It's lit beyond belief.'

Mark nods.

'It's so fire, so lit,' Father LeBron says, 'this coffee. It's like when the University of Illinois Fighting Illini Football team, many years ago, tried to get recruiting hype by claiming their team resided in quote, "Littyville," but then they opened that season, whatever that season was, by almost losing to like Toledo or something and, man, the fans were so, so angry. Like, wow, we come up with this cringe "Littyville" thing and to back up that swagger you gotta be like the Miami Hurricanes[49] of the early 90s or early 2000s, the U, that kind of thing, but here we are going full swagger and almost losing to Toledo. But this

---

[49] It's too bad the legend of Reese Poffenbarger didn't include a Miami season with a stat sheet like 4,556 yds passing, 51 TDs against only 6 INTs, maybe an additional 400 yards on the ground and 7 TDs (a lot of QB sneak/pile pushes from inside the 1 yard line).

coffee, I mean this coffee is actually Littyville.'

Mark nods, again, Mark refills his cup and will soon be onto a third maybe a fourth.

Anna is standing alone by the window looking out at the rain, rain, rain, rain coming down in sheets, the rain.

Her mind wanders to the Book of Genesis.

She hears the words bubble up inside her, as if on their own.

11 In the six hundredth year of Noah's life, on the seventeenth day of the second month—on that day all the springs of the great deep burst forth, and the floodgates of the heavens were opened. And rain fell on the earth forty days and forty nights.[50]

---

[50] Genesis, 7:11–12.

Chastity

'How many inches do you think have fallen already?'
Mark asks.

'Feet,' Father LeBron says.

'Feet? It's only been raining since last night.'

'Feet,' he says again. 'About two feet.'

'So, the Old Moscow Pullman Highway is going to
flood?' Anna asks.

'It already has.'

'Has? It's already flooded?'

She walks over to the window to get a better look.
It's hard to see the road, the ground, because it's coming
down so hard. The rain is torrential, tropical, monsoon
season set on cruise control, auto-pilot.

'Soaked,' Father LeBron says. 'It's wetter than wading
fifteen feet into the Atlantic Ocean. The sogginess factor is Eastern Iowa after a week of intermittent squalls
concluding in three hours and thirteen minutes of it's
coming down so hard it looks like it's coming *up* from
the pavement. You go walk on that,' he points out the
window, 'you're soon sinking, sinking, gurgling on down,
sinking fast.'

'Quagmire,' Mark says.

'Bog-marsh,' Father LeBron replies.

'Fever swamp city in Northwest Louisiana,' Marks adds.

'South of Shreveport,' Father Lebron says, going along
with the impromptu theme. 'Cajun dialects for many
miles before you reach New Orleans.'

'The Passchendaele battlefield during the Third Ypres
campaign in autumn, 1917,' Mark says.

'Now,' Father LeBron says, nodding his head and taking

a deep drink of his coffee. It's even close to a pull, a pull draft-drag on the coffee. 'Now we're getting somewhere, yes, towards some kind of understanding.'

'Okay,' Anna says, 'so what do we do then? What now?'

'I already told you. We finish the spiritual directing. As we're doing that the guys show up, the ice shows up, then the whole big thing happens, at the end. But it's not the End Times, we also talked about that. We talk about Chastity, proto-Protestants, Time. Afterwards, I mean in the aftermath, you guys write your book and.... um...well, uh, I'll just leave the rest to the realm of mystery. God is in control, so leave it be. Let's us, all of us, leave it at that. But it's really, really cool. Trust me. Okay?'

'Ok,' Anna says, pouring herself a cup of coffee and sitting down. She sits down in an inviting way, in a way that declares, without words, that this is the place to be, come. So they do—Mark and Father LeBron.

'Guys,' the priest says. 'What if this time, unlike the previous three times, we just got to it? I'm mean got right to it, after it? We're always hanging out, first, eating good food, first, deadlifting and singing and me waiting for you guys to arrive by plane, by train, by car, from afar, first, by that I mean beforehand. But, look, you're here. And hear, hear: here you're going to be until the getting done of this thing that needs to be done gotten is have been begotten done. So, what do you say, shall we?'

'Yes,' Anna says, pen in hand again, pen tapping on that one and same notebook yet again. 'Yes. Let's keep this momentum going. Mark?' she looks at her husband.

'Yeah,' he says, finishing off the hazelnut mocha with a visible finality that will ensure Father LeBron will soon have to strike up another pot or sit there thinking about the reality that, yes, and no doubt: there is no coffee left.

'Yeah,' Mark says, now sitting down. 'Cool, yeah, whatever.'

Father LeBron lights a pipe. Puffs,
       puffs,

       puffs

       and then snaps his fin-
       gers as he leans in, leans
       forward, and says:

'Okay, Chastity.
My lesson will come in three parts.

A. What Saint Augustine said.
B. Chronicling the Cringe, with a (parenthetical note
   'so as to reject it').
C. Positive prescriptions

.51

---

[51] This is a period. You are seeing that correctly. Hence why the next sentence starts with a capital letter.

One, what Saint Augustine said,' Father Lebron now is smoking two pipes at once and his entire face is covered in thick, billowy smoke. It's riding the fine line, the over-electrified fence, between very cool and very creepy. Like when you see a guy at the gym working out in a ski mask. That Father LeBron just keeps on speaking through the smoke, not coughing, not bothered by a veritable titanic smokestack level of smoke right in his face, is peculiar. Suffice to say: Mark has never seen a man smoke two pipes at the same time, but: duh.

'Wait, can you repeat that?' Mark asks. Whatever Father LeBron had said after 'One, what Saint Augustine said...' Mark had been thinking about the pipes and the ski mask.

'Yes,' he says, 'One, what Saint Augustine said. I then started reading the first of his quotes, ...you ready now?"

Mark nods. Father LeBron speaks. 'So yeah, quotes[52], I'll read his quotes and then add commentary where needed and when necessary. I want you to imagine the quotes are themselves basted and covered, I'm talking like down to even the

I

N

D

I

V

I

D

U

A

L

---

[52] McShaunessaey, *The Interconnected Web-Currents of Saint Augustine of Hippo's Thought*, 96–101; St. Augustine, *Confessions* (Oxford: Oxford University Press, trans. Henry Chadwick, 1991), III, iii; 38; St. Augustine, *Confessions*, II, xi, 32; St. Augustine, *Confessions*, IV, x; St. Augustine, *Confessions*, VIII, vii, 144–45.

letters,
in a yellowly-like butterscotch-buttermilk Werther's original color.

Because they're rich, and when properly understood, tastily beneficial such as
this. Okay?'

Mark and Anna nod. Anna closes her eyes momentarily to try and imagine the proper color. Father Lebron begins.

1. The more unscrupulous I was, the greater my reputation was likely to be, for men are so blind that they even take pride in their blindness.

    —'How true for those caught in the snares of sexual sin,' Father LeBron says. 'I was watching a video once about a priest talking about his life before becoming a priest and the talk was about chastity and he said quote, "I struggled a lot in the area before becoming a priest," and one of the top commentators said, "what a humble flex that is." And, yeah, how sad is that? Now I'm not going to pass judgement on this priest; his intentions, why he said this, it could have been that: that he wanted to establish something like street cred by letting his audience know, "hey, I'm no prude," and if it's that, then how sad is that? There's actually nothing cool about having hooked up with a bunch of people in the past. We do however, like Augustine says, take pride in it. "I'm good now, I've changed and repented, now, but before, I was with like 50 women, wait, 60, actually, maybe it was close to 100." Even those wanting to be on the path towards holiness take pride in that, they like hearing that, find that to be validation and some kind of badge of honor. For, as the great saint says, there is a joy in doing the wrong simply for its own sake.'

2. What an abomination! What a parody of life! What abysmal death! Could I enjoy doing wrong for no other reason than that it was wrong?

    'Indeed, anyone caught in these snares, these webs of falsehoods, comes to realize that and the following:'

3. Even though it clings to things of beauty, if their beauty is outside God and outside the soul, it only clings to sorrow.

4. The truth, of course, was that it was all my own self, and my own impiety had divided me against myself. My sin was all the more incurable because I did not think myself a sinner.

5. I lived in misery, like every man whose soul is tethered by the love of things that cannot last and then is
agonized to lose them.

6. But my sin was this, that I looked for pleasure, beauty,
and truth not in Him but in myself and his other
creatures, and the search led me instead to pain, confusion, and error.

'So, there you have it, those six. Sit with those six,'
Father LeBron says. 'If I could distill them into a bite
size portion of wisdom it would be something like this:
sin and sinful behaviors, especially in the realm of sexual
sin, are loved by their practitioners for the sake of the
sin itself, for the transgression and the pleasure, and
doing them, let us not kid ourselves, can bring one much
worldly acclaim and backslapping stamps of approval. But,
vanity of vanities, it leads, ultimately, and maybe even
in the here and now by ways of diseases, broken relationships, shattered families, betrayals, and the bitterest,
worm-wooded jealousies into pain, confusion, error, and
sorrow. Augustine knew, he knew he had to change, but,
like us, like all of us, and so what a great saint for us,
all of us, made one of the most human prayer requests
in all of history, a quote as famous as his "our heart is
restless..."[53] when he prayed,'

---

[53] Arguably Saint Augustine's most famous quote, it is part of the opening paragraph to his grand spiritual autobiography/(what we would call
today) 'faith testimony' and, in context, is found as such, *emphasis* mine:

'You are great, Lord, and highly to be praised (Ps: 47:2): great is your
power and your wisdom is immeasurable (Ps 146:5). Man, a little piece of
your creation, desires to praise you, a human being "bearing his mortality
with him" (2 Cor. 4:10), carrying with him the witness of his sin and the
witness that you "resist the proud" (I Pet. 5:5). Nevertheless, to praise
you is the desire of man, a little piece of creation. You stir man to take
pleasure in praising you, **because you have made us for yourself, and
our heart is restless until it rests in you.**'

—*Confessions* and (St. Augustine, *Confessions*, Book I, trans. Chadwick, 1991, 3)

7. Grant me chastity, Lord, just not yet.

'God,' Father LeBron says, 'was patient with Saint Augustine as He is patient with all of us, ready to welcome us home whenever we too are ready to respond to that voice telling us to "take up and read."

And so, post conversion, Augustine could write in reference to his now properly orientated desire for love:'

8. All my empty dreams suddenly lost their charm and my heart began to throb with a bewildering passion for the wisdom of eternal truth.

'and,'

9. To fall in love with God is the greatest romance; to seek Him is the greatest adventure; to find Him, the greatest human achievement.

'Amen,' Father LeBron says, 'that's that, and good stuff, that. 9 excellent quotes that can tell us so much, and but 9 amongst an easy 900 you could rack up, and on so many diverse   topics, for such was the mind of this great saint, so illuminated by God's grace. Also, and by the way, Camus was totally right about the condition of his society then, the 1940s and 50s, and what was true then is so much more true now.

Page 10 into page 11 of the Foio Collection, publishing house Gallimard, but of course, in his grand but largely overshadowed book *La Chute*.'

Je reve parfois de ce que diront de nous les historiens futurs. Une phrase leur suffira pour l'homme modern: il forniquait et lisait les journaux. Apres cette forte definition, le sujet sera, si j'ose dire, épuisé.[54]

---

[54] Camus, *La Chute* (Editions Gallimard, 1956, pps 10–11).

'Amazing,' Father LeBron says, 'right? I mean, spot on.'
Anna nods in agreement.

Mark does nothing. Does not motion or make any
noise. He doesn't speak French.

'Except,' Anna says, '...and scrolled endlessly though
internet pages, or...and played video games. I mean
whatever the attractive-attaching whatever is for us and
those in the future. You know, everything we talked about
last time.'

'Yes,' Father LeBron says. 'Well done, brilliant even.
Okay, Let us now pass on to—

B. Chronicling the Cringe, with a (parenthetical note "so as to reject it")

Father LeBron exhales; smoke. He then puts both pipes away, simultaneously. He then picks up what has got to be a 40, wait, maybe 50 ounce glass of beer, and he starts chugging away and if it's the former, now it's about 23 ounces, if the latter, 33.

'Sorry,' he says. 'Wait,' putting down the mug. 'Okay, okay. Look, I just cannot, I cannot talk about Catholics and chastity and by chastity we're of course talking about sex, so I cannot talk about Catholics and sex in a normal, conversational way. There's too much cringe. This section is about chronicling the cringe so I can only do that by way of either bullet points, and even listing the numbers therein, or by way of Dante-inspired *terza rima* poetry. Okay? Are you guys cool with that?'

Mark and Anna nod.
Anna: you already know she's taking and has been taking notes,
 notes,
 notes,
 notes,
 notes.

"Okay,' Father Lebron says,

I am LeBron,[55]   193
I am Lebron,
Lebron I am.

That Lebron-I-Am
That LeBron-I-Am
I do not like that Lebron-I-Am

Do you like to listen to Catholic chastity speakers?
I do not like them, Lebron-I-Am   200
   I do not like how cringy, and yucky their phraseology, so full of
cheese and ham . . .

I do like to hear them in the house
I do not like to see them with a mouse
I do not like their talks or books here or there
I do not like them anywhere   205

'Wait,
wait,
wait,' Father LeBron says, stopping. He picks up the
mug and chugs a lug-lugs, again. 'Sorry. Never mind, Let's
start over. . . . .

   Uh . . . .
. . . .
. . . .
. . . .
. . . .
. . . .
. . . .
. . . .
. . . .
. . . .
. . . .
. . . .

---

[55] Please see, because a play/parody/homage on/of/to: Dr. Suess, *Green Eggs and Ham* (New York: Random House, 1960).

'let's try bullet points. Imagine them big,
massive-big font in front of you.'

1. Chastity is super important. Wait till you're married. Be faithful to your spouse. Be open to life.

'Guys, crushing! This is it, this is the advice. It was bullet point one but it's such a good summation let's make it two too:'

2. Chastity is super important. Wait till you're married. Be faithful to your spouse. Be open to life.

'Do those four and you'll be doing very, very well. Fully Catholic, fully rational, fully happy, just excellent. Ah, why not, (?), why not (?) make it bullet point three, these four points, a final time:'

3. Chastity is
   super important.
   Wait till you're
   married.
   Be faithful to
   your spouse.
   Be open to life.

'So, yep,
   yep,
   look,

done.

I'm done with bullet points and we're not going to be needing Dante's *terza rima* helps, either, Dr. Suess did the trick. I wanted to roast the marshmallow a bit and, mission accomplished, it was about to fall off into the fire.'

Would you? Could you? Listen to their podcasts in a car?[56]   206
Listen! Listen! Here they are.

I would not, could not, in a car.

You may like them, you will see.
You might like a Catholic chastity conference held in a tree.

I would not, could not in a tree. `   211
Not in a car! You Let me be.
I do not like Catholic chastity books in a box.
I would like them to be eaten by a fox.

A train! A train! A train!
Could you, would you take a train
to that Catholic Chastity conference?   217

Not by way of train! Not in a tree!
Not in-car podcasting, Father LeBron I am, let me be!   219

---

56 Ibid.

'Sorry...,' Father LeBron says, 'but do you...do you know what I mean, am I, is this making sense? Something like 100% yes to the full Theology of the Body, Saint John Paul the Great sexual ethic. Yes, 100%, yes, those 4 points above. But so much, no, no, no, no, no to the way it's often delivered...it's so bad, so poorly...

'Yeah,' Mark says, 'Yeah, no, I totally get it. Can I, um, can I like take over? Like, add my thoughts here?'

'Go for it,' Father LeBron says, in a go for it way like *you do that and I'll then be able to get back to this beer* and so he does; that.

'Yeah,' Mark says. 'I know exactly what you mean. Live the Catholic sexual ethic then shut up, just

shut up.

If you want to encourage people to be chaste, and to help those poor people struggling with whatever type of sexual sins,

stop talking about it.

Some guy goes on some show and he's presented as an expert on this, or something, and immediately, you know, sorry, sorry for judging a book by its cover but you're like dude you've never even spoken to a real woman before, you know nothing, nothing about men and women and so whatever you're saying, I'm going to do the opposite. And when that happens, what a true tragedy, because the guy might be saying the actual correct things, like those four things you mentioned before, Father LeBron, well done, 100% agree, he might be saying things like that but in the worst, over the top, incredibly patronizing way. Like, there you go, there you go, that's at least a part of it. I don't know why, I mean you tell me, but Catholics have this really weird way of talking about sex that's like a combination of prudishness and Dad jokes. It's like, let's try to act like we're cool about sex but also, haha, sex, that guy just said sex, haha, and then it's like one of these Catholic guys actually had a video that was like prude/Dadjoke titled something like "How often should you and your wife, you know, you know." Like that was the actual title. And the only thought I had, seeing that, was that you people, you and your wife, should never do that, live as brother and sister, 100%, it should be illegal for you two to ever do that, and wow, you're really ruining all this for everyone, cringing it up in that prudish, sex, haha, sex, way. Just
shut up!

Some lady went on this show once and the show was like
one of these Catholic shows online, you know what I mean,
but so they got to talking about Theology of the Body stuff
and the host and the lady, his guest, were talking about
early marriage and the transition into years of marriage
and just so many cliches and then the lady and the guy
started like getting stuck on something like, quote,

"haha, you know, haha, sex, haha, like you know when
you're first married and all you care about is getting sex,
haha, sex, haha"

and it was so utterly, impossibly, insufferable. I thought, as
she was saying this, lady, look, you and your husband are
like the two most legit and certified obnoxious people on
the face of the earth. Anyone watching this and thinking
about maybe becoming Catholic and discerning marriage
and being chaste and then having a Catholic marriage and
then a Catholic family—praise God, all these wonderful,
wonderful things—is going to be put off from doing all
of it, because of your stupid, immature, sex, haha, sex,
type testimonial. Just

shut up.
Shut up.

And wow, guys,' Mark points to Anna and Father LeBron, 'forgive me for this long rant, I promise I almost done. But it's like Walker Percy said at some point in his book *Lost in the Cosmos*,[57] you know, the last self-help book, lol, a parody of self-help and all that because the only and final answer is Christ Himself. So self-help apart from this, Him, is a joke. But so Percy said that how often does it turn out the person at the conference who's the star of the conference and is going on and on about the importance of this and those and these kinds of tips concerning being pure in relationships is, behind closed doors, doing very much the opposite? So, whenever some huge sex scandal breaks out about some pastor and everyone is so, so shocked, I'm just saying, I'm not. Saint Augustine, right, Father Lebron? Concupiscence. Maybe those loudest and most consistent are, I don't know, trying to compensate for more concupiscence. I don't know. I do just wish more people would

shut up,

---

[57] Walker Percy, *Lost in the Cosmos* (New York: FSG, 1983).

just shut up.'

'Dang,' Father LeBron says, 'I mean. You got after it a bit there. Kind of harsh, don't you think? Tell me how you really feel next time,' he says, laughing.

'Fine,' Mark says, 'but you agree with me, right?'

Father LeBron nods and bites on his pipe, re-lit. 'Yeah, much of that, sure, I suppose I do. What do you think, Anna?'

'I like Catholic conferences,' she says. 'Chastity speakers, chastity speakers going on those shows and stuff Mark talked about. They're good, I think. I mean, look,' she says, popping an enormous pink bubble of some type of chewing gum. She gnaws down on it, pop, pop again, nods and continues. 'I mean someone has got to do it, right? What? Just let like, what, the secular, um, the secular culture or something dictate the norms and mores of sexual stuff, stuff broadly speaking? No, we need these people, cheesy or not. They're good.'

'Okay,' Father LeBron says, sending skyward, up towards the roof then puff, dissipation, gone

his most impressive smoke ring yet. Man, this priest
loves to drink,

smoke,

    deadlift

and

    dunk.

He's gotta, Mark's been thinking this, and for a while
now, man, he's gotta make a video where he just

smokes up his face to where you can't see him,

like before,
and it's just an insane amount of

smoke smoke smoke smoke smoke smoke smoke smoke
smoke smoke smoke smoke smoke smoke smoke smoke
smoke smoke smoke smoke smoke smoke smoke smoke
smoke smoke smoke smoke smoke smoke smoke smoke
smoke smoke smoke smoke smoke smoke smoke smoke
smoke smoke smoke smoke smoke smoke smoke smoke
smoke smoke smoke smoke smoke smoke smoke smoke
smoke smoke smoke smoke smoke smoke smoke smoke
smoke smoke smoke smoke smoke smoke smoke smoke
smoke smoke smoke smoke smoke smoke smoke smoke
smoke smoke smoke smoke smoke smoke smoke smoke
smoke smoke smoke smoke smoke smoke smoke smoke
smoke smoke smoke smoke smoke smoke smoke smoke
smoke smoke smoke smoke smoke smoke smoke smoke
smoke smoke smoke smoke smoke smoke smoke smoke
smoke smoke smoke smoke smoke smoke smoke smoke
smoke smoke smoke smoke smoke smoke smoke smoke
smoke smoke smoke smoke smoke smoke smoke smoke
smoke smoke smoke smoke smoke smoke smoke smoke
smoke smoke smoke smoke smoke smoke smoke smoke
smoke smoke smoke smoke smoke smoke smoke smoke
smoke smoke smoke smoke smoke smoke smoke smoke
smoke smoke smoke smoke smoke smoke smoke smoke
smoke smoke smoke smoke smoke smoke smoke smoke
smoke smoke smoke smoke smoke smoke smoke smoke
smoke smoke smoke smoke smoke smoke smoke smoke
smoke smoke smoke smoke smoke smoke smoke smoke
smoke smoke smoke smoke smoke smoke smoke smoke
smoke smoke smoke smoke smoke smoke smoke smoke
smoke smoke smoke smoke smoke smoke smoke smoke

smoke smoke smoke smoke smoke smoke smoke smoke
smoke smoke smoke smoke smoke smoke smoke smoke
smoke smoke smoke smoke smoke smoke smoke smoke
smoke smoke smoke smoke smoke smoke smoke smoke
smoke smoke smoke smoke smoke smoke smoke smoke
smoke smoke smoke smoke smoke smoke smoke smoke
smoke smoke smoke smoke smoke smoke smoke smoke
smoke smoke smoke smoke smoke smoke smoke smoke
smoke smoke smoke smoke smoke smoke smoke smoke
smoke smoke smoke smoke smoke smoke smoke smoke
smoke smoke smoke smoke smoke smoke smoke smoke
smoke smoke smoke smoke smoke smoke smoke smoke
smoke smoke smoke smoke smoke smoke smoke smoke
smoke smoke smoke smoke smoke smoke smoke smoke

and then it clears and he dunks from the foul line and
then hangs on the rim, chills there, while some dude
climbs a ladder and just starts dumping gallons of beer
all over him.

'Mark, you got anything? What do you think?'

'Wait, what?'
Mark says. 'Sorry. Was zoning out there a bit, my bad.'

'I was asking: so what would you do then?,' Father LeBron
says. 'Positive prescriptions, man. I hit you with the

A. Saint Augustine.

I tried to re-rock on

B. see: chronicling the cringe.

But I couldn't. I kind of failed, sorry, went off
on a few of those Dr. Suess sidetracks. But you,
harsh though it may have been, you came to
the rescue. So, bring it home.

C. Positive Prescriptions. Let's wrap this up.'

Mark exhales.

'Okay, yeah, sure. Let's number them too. I like how you do that,' he says to Father LeBron. 'But I want you, in your mind's eye to imagine my numbers, my points, in 40 point font... okay? So, yeah, yeah, fine. I go on one of these shows. Number 0 for me, the foundational thing, would be

to be aloof. A good

aloof, not like arrogance or I think I'm better than you, than this, I mean like I freaking hate how everyone overshares. *Oh, I'm just so happy to be here, I'm such a fan of your show, ow wow, oh man, so, like, wow, here's everything about me and all my thoughts and this is so cool*... just shut that BS down immediately. You have to overcorrect. Chesterton said the saint has to be the antidote, the antivenom. So, 0: you gotta go on and be like, basically, I'm doing you the favor being on this stupid show. Not only am I not that happy to be here, when are we wrapping this up? You gotta give one word answers.

Yes.
    No.
        I don't know.
        Nah.
            Yep.
                None of your business.

Especially that last one—I'm assuming here in this hypothetical you're going on to speak about chastity—you gotta answer all the cringe bait questions about you and your wife with non-answers.

For example,

Q. So tell me about how you and your wife met.
A. No.

Q. What's one thing, you really love, just love, about your
wife?
A. Don't worry about it.

And dude, bro, man, wow, you do the opposite of that lady before. The host asks you about sex, any like personal questions in this regard, just say nothing. Make him feel like an idiot for even asking. So, okay, you keep on the o. approach and the mystique you're building, probably like 20 minutes in, is insane. The audience, even the interviewer, have been won over by you. *Wow, wait, this guy, and he's Catholic, why is he 0% cringe (?), did he really just cancel cringe in 20 minutes? He's the man. Everyone who comes on this show seems so friendly and nice in the most vomit inducing way. I think this guy actually hates us and I don't know why, but I love it, I love that.* So once you've got them in the palm of your hand you do the one through four thing we repeated above three times: Chastity is super important. Wait till you're married. Be faithful to your spouse. Be open to life. There's five things already: 0, 1, 2, 3, 4.

Number 5. Read
Theology of the
Body for sure.
Both: the real one[58]
and the Christo-
pher West one too,[59]
the Theology of the
Body for dummies.
6. When you're
engaged, do the

---

[58] John Paul II, *The Theology of the Body: Human Love in the Divine Plan* (Alexandria, VA: Pauline Books and Media, 1997).

[59] Christopher West, *Theology of the Body for Beginners: A Basic Introduction to Pope John Paul II's Sexual Revolution* (West Chester, PA: Ascension Press, 2004).

Pre-Cana classes. They're really valuable for going into marriage with your feet on the ground, clear eyed, well prepared. 7. Finally, a last thing I'd say, is just be normal about sex.

It's as normal as brushing your teeth, growing old, and chronic lower back pain. Just,

shut up.

Catholics, a lot of us it seems to me anyways, demonize it, or put in on a pedestal, obsess about it, both good and bad, and cringe out about it so, so prodigiously. So, I'd probably come back to that: shut up.

Shut up

Shut up

Shut up.

Just,

shut up.'

A silence descends on the room.   220
Fog, an eerie fog, greenish like in advance of a Tornado
on the Plains
has itself descended upon
the Old Moscow Pullman Highway.   225

The rain is gone but they had not noticed until now that the ice
has arrived.
Everything,
all of it,
all of however how much had fallen was now
frozen.

Just like the good priest had said it would be,
it was.   233

Too late.[60]
Mark's queen, Anna, is caught between why am I here?
and, wow,
but this is cool. To be caught up in so grand and maybe glorious
an adventure.

She feeds these thoughts within her veins.
She is eaten by a secret flame. Mark's   240
high name, all he has done, again, again,
come like a flood.
His face—what a model, he, just like
her, she,
wow, the two of us, she thinks,
soon blushing at such a sudden outbreak of pride.   246

A new dawn might soon light the earth,
Anna thinks.
Banishing damp shadows from the sky
when restless Dido turns to her heart's sharer:
'Anna, my sister, what dreams make me shudder?
Who is this stranger guest come to our house?
How confident he looks, how strong his chest
and arms!'   254

---

[60] Virgil, *The Aeneid* (trans. Mandelbaum), Book IV, 79.

You know, Anna thinks to herself, she's right, Dido, if Dido was her sister because Dido did have a sister named Anna. She's right, Dido, talking about Aeneas, his confidence and strength. She smiles, Anna does, because Mark is checking those boxes too. It's good to be married. Good to be married to him.

It's so pretty outside the window, heavily frosted, all that water, yep, yep, it sure is. Quite frozen. Anna smiles again, thinking back to the first time her grandfather took her skating on a frozen pond many Christmases ago. How nice that would be now, to lace them up, and click, clack, slide and glide all over the

Old Moscow Pullman Highway.

5

Donatism and Proto-Protestantism

The rain that had fallen with terrifying speed and turned to ice hours before seemed to further harden before Anna's eyes. Like it was setting into place, bracing internally, like concrete. It appeared to get shinier, too, crystallizing clean like a fine pane of glass upon which some powdered sugar had lately spilled. And you swept, swept, swept if off to find beneath translucence, transparency, and proper conduits for effulgent light just about begging to be set into motion into action—see: a flashlight clicked ON—so as to exit out and pass through, almost instantaneously.

Anna kept on hugging her warm, steam emitting from the top,

cup.

A sweet steam it smelled so good as it leapt up directly from an amalgamated pomegranate, orange, and chamomile steep, the

three in one

long soaking into a unity, hardly even the palest image of the

Ultimate Form

of it, but such is

God's

good sense of humor—leaving us clues and helps ever along the way.

That scented, flavored steam went directly up Anna's nose and hit some notes somewhere higher still, in what must have then been beyond the frontier of 'nose' and into the region of
'brain.'

It was very nice, that was for sure, and Anna wished she could be out there, on the lately called Old Moscow Pullman Highway she had come to love, no doubt, but which had been transformed into a new creation. To touch it, the ice, glide ungloved fingers across it, bounce firm fingernails up and down on it like playing the piano, the sounds, the feel, the sky, the cold, the windows, the now fully frosted over windows. She sat down and kept looking out the window, remembering to take a sip of her tea every now and then.

Speaking of bracing internally, Father LeBron had told Mark that that was the most important part of the deadlift movement. Set up with the bar mid foot, bend over and grab it just outside the feet, the feet pointed out a bit, then drop down into place keeping the hips high,
fine,
fine,
fine.

All this was good and true, but the key was the internal brace, right after you shook the slack out of the bar, the brace initiated with a firm exhale and then you were just about ready to go: eyes straight ahead, push the floor away from you with as much leg drive as you can muster.

Father LeBron was, right now, as Anna looked out through the frosted window past the steam coming off her cup, hitting an 815 triple, with plans to cool down to the tune of one set of 5 at 600, and as many reps as possible, as explosively as possible, at 315. Then, he had told them, we'll begin our 5th, and penultimate, spiritual advising lesson. On, 'Donatism and Proto-Protestantism,' he had told them, whatever that meant.

'You sure you don't want to tell us what's going to happen?' Mark says to Father Lebron.

'Nah.'

'Really?'

'Yep.'

'So, no? No, you are not going to tell us.'

'Nah.'

'Why?'

'Don't want to.'

'Really?'

'Yeah. Don't want to. So, no. But guys,' Father LeBron says, to both Mark and Anna. 'You have to trust God, trust in His Providence. And doing so know that you have free will. You're not puppets on a string here, or anything like that, no one is. God's will can be thwarted. Why? God willed that His will could be thwarted. God desires that all men, ALL men, ALL PEOPLE, be saved.[61] But some, we know, are not. We know Hell is real and that some people go to Hell. C. S. Lewis—since we're going to be talking about Protestants and the like in this fifth session—said, I'm paraphrasing, said something like, 'the door to hell is closed from within.'[62] That, and God's will being thwarted, and why you're not puppets, same thing, same reason: free will. God willed that people have free will and so we do. Don't let anyone tell you differently.

God has a plan for you,

---

[61] 1 Timothy 2:3-4.
[62] C. S. Lewis, *The Great Divorce* (London: Geoffrey Bles, 1945).

and if you fulfill that plan you will be happy. If you don't, you will not

be happy.

But it's your

choice.

God will give you all the grace, every ounce of it, to complete the task he has set out for you from time immemorial. But then you gotta activate the thing he has given you reign over to activate or de-activate, you gotta push that free will button, and get-getting to work, get-getting the job done.

Listen to Saint Augustine on free will. What hogwash, what B. S., some Protestants verifiably bathe in who claim that Saint Augustine denied free will. What utter be-clownification.

Listen,

to Saint Augustine.

'As He is the Creator of all natures, so He is the giver of all powers—though He is not the maker of all choices...God knows all things before they happen; yet we act by choice in all those things where we feel and know that we cannot act otherwise than willingly...that fact is that our choices fall within the order of the causes which is known for certain to God and is contained in His foreknowledge—for human choices are the causes of human acts...Our conclusion is that our wills have the power to do all that God wanted them to do and foresaw they could do.'[63]

---

[63] Saint Augustine, *City of God*, Book V, (that real copy) 106–108.

Meanwhile Mark, well upon his way[64]   255
to check on Father LeBron still lifting steadfast, cutting
through the ribbons of personal PRs completed beneath this cold
wind, gazing,
Mark was, at how easily the priest moved 600 pounds like trumpets
against the walls
of Jericho, again, his once thought limitations now glowing,
gone up in the flames of
triumph.   261

But the walls of Carthage never glowed
with the love Anna had for Mark, and Mark for her. Neither of
whom can know
what caused so vast a blaze,
and here, in this very place, on that first date many days
ago.
Yet the models, all models
know well the pain when passion is profaned
and how men and women driven wild can act.
Their hearts drawn through dark presentiments
declaring St. Paul's own words to be ever true: better marry than be on
                                                                         271
fire.

'You guys ready for our next to last lesson?'
Father LeBron called out. The final weight clanking to the floor a final
time.
Pious Mark answered from the doorway in between the priest,
within his makeshift gym, and his wife,
by the window, looking out a type of looking glass at the glassy
Ice.   279

'Even I
have seen the reason, long since this began, this, what the winds
demand, these lessons, with you, Father. And that it is useless now
to struggle.
Anna, my daring, let then our course be like our sails. For can any
country please me more

---

[64] Virgil, *The Aeneid* (trans. Mandelbaum), Book V, 103–04.

or offer me more welcome harbor than
the land that now holds us captive, the Palouse, this dirt and these hills,
and who knows for how long.   287
God knows.
'God's will be done.'

For Mark and Anna kind winds even indoors seem to swell
their sails; the fleet runs swift across the surge;
At last, and glad, they reach familiar sands:
Sitting down, drinks the three
of them,
in hand,
ready to begin the nearly final

Lesson.   297

On, 'Donatism and Proto-Protestantism,' Father LeBron says, having emerged from somewhere in the restaurant/ house/the place (this place) [the one and only one as it is and has been the whole time] wearing a white, scientist's/ doctor's coat, pushing a cart on top of which is an old school projector, pushing the cart with his left hand while he holds a reel of film in his right hand.

'Yeah,' he says, plugging it in, setting it up. 'Yeah, you all ready for round 5?'

I nod.
I look over at Mark but
he's not paying attention. Probably thinking about me.
I smile.
I hope neither of them noticed me smile.
I wish men were different but if they were different, I wouldn't like that. Only other women can understand what I mean by this. I don't like that he's never paying attention, and that I have to tell him nine times and then a tenth, and that even then he still forgets, and that he can't even do the 10% of things around the house that I ask him to do, all the lesser things, and they're the same things the whole time because men can't handle curveballs, they're like dogs, they need the same thing, the same way, all the time, or it all gets messed up. But every time I start to get angry, I realize he's not thinking about the thing he's supposed to be thinking about because he's thinking about me. Women do not understand, I mean they do not even begin to understand until they've been around a man long enough, that men really are thinking about women all the time. Women, we, we are not think-ing about men all the time. This is not a two-way street. There are chores to do, a 50% sale on this and that but only this weekend, should I use eggshell white,

white dove,
simply white,
snowbound,
or
Swiss coffee
paint for the downstairs bathroom? Where are my slippers,
      please don't use that blanket, I put my face on
      that blanket,
      are you sure it tastes okay,

                                                  (?)

      are you mad at me,

                                                  (?)

      do you hate my sister, no, but really, where are my
                                       slippers
                                                (?)

    Men think about nothing but food, women, sports,
money and, maybe, sometimes working out and videos
of other men working out. Cars too. But mostly

                  women.

    And Mark is thinking about me, me!, can you believe it?
      Me! Believe
      me,

it doesn't matter if you're considered the most beautiful
woman in the world or you're some girl in the middle of
nowhere with zero self-confidence and shoes two sizes too

big and when you laugh you snort and you really hate
that about yourself, if the guy you like likes you, you love
that. And then, at that moment, becoming aware that he
likes you, God willing later on loves and cherishes you, all,
all I tell you, is forgiven. So, if Mark actually did everything on time like some kind of in-house butler-bot it
would mean he would never be off daydreaming about me.
And I would hate that. That's what I mean, that's what I
mean that only a woman can understand me when I say,
once more, I wish men were different, but if they were
different I wouldn't like that. And then—

'Anna,' Mark says. 'Anna.'
I must have visibly shook my head for I can feel my
eyes recoiling back into focus the way you do when waking
suddenly. I guess I was really out of it.
'Anna,' he says again.
'Yeah, what? What?'
'Are you cool with that? Are you okay if Father LeBron
turns on the projector and we begin the next lesson?'
'Umm.... —
Mark shakes his head. 'Women,' he says to Father
LeBron.
Father LeBron nods back approvingly.
'They're the worst,' Mark says. 'That dude, whoever he
was, was right: can't live with 'em, can't live without 'em.'

I laugh. 'Yes, I'm ready,' tapping my ever-faithful note-book, ready for more blue ink to be pressed done in cal-ligraphous, careful attention to detail, swirls and swipes.

'Please,'
      I say,
'go
ahead.'

. . . .

I know, okay, I like, I like, um, like everything about Mark. Fine. But, I really like how good he is at this. This, like, um, like trolling me. He's so very good at it and it's actually very hard to do. To actually disrespect a woman and be mean to her, oh, no, I wish all the men in the world knew that. No woman likes that. To be demeaned, 'put in her place,' treated like she's less than.

No.

I have honestly never met a single gal, even very tradi-tional ones, who tell me in that no holds barred, woman to woman, heart to heart talks, that they like that. Conversely, if a man tries too hard around her: really, really wants to show what a gentleman he is and is overly nice and trying too hard to pay attention and yes-manning all her talking points, she's going to friend zone him pretty quick. I wish guys knew this too. Once a girl puts you in the friend zone your relationship is basically dinosaurs about to take direct hits to the face from meteors. It's extinction level event stuff, you're not coming back from that.

I'm smiling again. I hope they
don't see that I'm smiling.
See?

Mark is so great; of course, only a man would put it
like that. Dinosaurs taking direct hits to the face from
meteors. His phrase. He's 100 percent right. Demean a
woman, treat her like dirt, it's not going to work. Try too
hard, you get friend zoned, not going to work. It's about
balance. It's about, well, this is why I love the Catholic
faith. See the Book of Genesis, see John Paul II. Men and
women are equals, complimentary parts, partners in the
fullest sense, best friends, that's how it should be anyways
if you want it to
work.

So this is what I mean by how good Mark is at trolling
me. He kids me, prods me, makes me feel like he has 100%
self-confidence and I'm the one who should be nervous
around him, like he's in control, and I loved that from
the first date, from the first moment of the first date,
and it was an immediate anti-friend zone vaccine, it was
great. But then having done this, he's free to be a true
gentleman, and gentle with me, and to love on me, and
cherish me. And he does. It's like, hmm, it's like, uh, I
think women want this. They want a man who

puts God first,
then people next: them, their women, and of course their
children, their family, and just
all people.

Women want a man who puts God first,
                              others second,
                              himself

                              (sometimes even a distant)

third.

And they want a man to be kind, and nice, and funny, and just not Mr. Friendzone because that is just about the worse. Like, uh, be nice and sweet but also have the confidence that if I asked you to fight every man in the world shirtless in the middle of the street to prove your love to me—Middle Age knights jousting for maiden's scarves style—um, you would. So—

'Anna,' Mark says, once more breaking me out of it. 'Can we put the movie on?'
'Yes,' I say. 'Yes, please.'

The film turns on with a slow and rickety click. A hiccup, hiccup, screen to black, quick bright light, a flash, hiccup, a black screen for 2 seconds again, more clicks, and then, a man, someone out of the 1950s prototypical style—let's just say Rod Serling, cigarette in hand, black and white *Twlight Zone* opening—walks up and looks at you, the viewer, and says:
Read the following and commit it to memory.
He says this three times.
And it said, to sum it up, something basically like this, this film, the tenor of it, all of
it
said, rather
read,
as the following.

1st, there was a huge, centered citation, from a 1967 master's thesis written by Benjamin J. Hubbard and it looked like this:

ST. AUGUSTINE'S NOTION

OF

PENANCE AND RECONCILIATION

WITH THE CHURCH

by

Benjamin J. Hubbard, Jr., B.A.

A Thesis submitted to the Faculty of the

Graduate School, Marquette University

[65]

in Partial Fulfillment of the Requirements for the

Degree of Master of Arts

Milwaukee, Wisconsin April, 1967

---

[65] Benjamin J. Hubbard, Jr. *St Augustine's Notion of Penance and Reconciliation with the Church* (Marquette University, Milwaukee, WI, 1967).

Then a longform note—one page—came onto the screen regarding the whole point of this fifth lesson: the Donatists, which, the slides explained, were a heretical fifth century sect in North Africa that became, for lack of a better word, the first Protestants, protesting against the Universal Church Christ Himself had established and against which the gates of Hell shall not prevail. The Donatists claimed a church community of visible saints, that only those already perfect on Earth were part of the 'true church' and that those who had fallen into apostasy, surrendering sacred vessels or books, for example, could not be re-admitted to communion nor validly bequeath the sacraments to the faithful. Augustine countered by explaining, among other things, that the personal holiness of the priest—whether he be saint or utter scoundrel— has zero bearing on the validity of the Sacraments. The Real Presence is the Real Presence all the same whether the priest is holy or in grave sin. Augustine argued that, of course, even the worst sinners, post the Sacrament of Reconciliation, could be fully re-admitted to communion. And Augustine explained that while on earth a church of perfect, visible saints is not possible. We all struggle on, hopefully towards paradise by the grace of God here, in this vale of tears, but together, as One Church, One Faith and Baptism, not the already elect and damned while still in the flesh; here. As St Monica spent decades praying for the conversion of her son, her son, as Bishop of Hippo from AD 395 on, spent the same time fighting the errors of the Donatists, a thoroughgoing one being their Protestant proclivity to reduce the universal to the local and particular.[66] Saint Augustine was fighting for the Church; One,

---

[66] Two thumbs down.

Holy, Catholic, and Apostolic. Donatists were fighting to purge from the 'true church,' as they saw it, all and any last remnants of their own, self-classified impurities, a 'true church' that just so happened to exist in a very small corner of the world, North Africa,[67] as a millennium and some years more still, Anglicans would claim that the true faith resided solely on the British Isles,[68] as more years ahead yet some Americans would claim that God has specially, as in exclusively and to the exclusion of others, blessed this small corner of the world, this small land.[69] Heresy always has that as a telltale sign: reduction of the universal to the small and tribal.

That was the end of the note and that note, the film projector showed, was not part of the Hubbard article. But this following, these slides—see and commit to memory—were. And that same man who had opened the proceedings said 'excerpts from Hubbard are presented unaffected. Just see them and do with them as you will. The goldmine is gilded beyond measure. You do not seek to improve gold. You just display it. Here are some quotes from Hubbard, displayed.'

---

[67] No different than all the dudes, the guys, the mecs, tous les potes, who claim a/the 'true church' is to be found only in this southwest corner of the northern half of the western edge of some random, rural county in Arkansas, Kansas, or (please no, please stop, not Nebraska, do not befoul beautiful I-80 West cruise control chillin 80 mph on a flat road paved smooth as butter pecan when milled nine times out of Lincoln to North Platte and not too longer after onto/into Wyoming, Nebraska) Nebraska.

[68] Lol.

[69] Ibid. (True, but still, 'Being an American is pretty sweet though right?' Mark once asked Anna when they were driving in the car, she driving, he picking out music, 'I hope "God bless America" goes, uh, to, to the maximum you know. I'm saying sign me up and Lord have mercy on us.' Anna nodded and tapped the steering wheel twice before turning on her turn signal to turn left. 'I really love Canada, Canadians,' she said. 'Especially the Western Provinces, except for British Columbia.'

Hence the sacraments give her visible character to the Church,

and in a sense build her up externally. Yet they also give
the Church her internal unity since they are indispensable for eternal
salvation and are not to be found outside of her.
The effect of these sacraments is indescribably great and to treat
them contemptuously is to be guilty of sacrilege. For to despise what
is indispensable for
complete union with God is to: become god- less (Q. Faustum Man-
ich. 19. 11).

Having already mentioned that the sacraments give internal unity
to the Church, we now turn specifically to Augustine's teaching
on the Church as the Body of Christ, as an invisible and spiritual
organization. The sacrament which most especially makes possible this
spiritual unity in Christ's Body is. of course, the Eucharist.
The Eucharist is our daily bread; and our power for good. which is
shown forth therein, is unity. That is to say that we are made into
his own body; and having been made into
his body, we ourselves become what we receive (Serm. 57. 7).[70]

Just as serious sin involves the loss of the life-giving Spirit, forgiveness
of sin involves the return of the Spirit. In fact, Augustine teaches that
it is through the Holy Spirit that sins are forgiven.
It is against this gratuitous gift, against this grace of God that the
impenitent heart speaks. Impenitence itself is then blasphemy of the
Spirit which finds remission neither in this life nor in the next.[71]

Again, Augustine closely identifies the Church ("rock," "unity") with
the Spirit ("dove") in the forgiveness of sins. He points out that the
Church's peace is necessary for forgiveness from God, and he states
that the Apostles represent the whole Church in their mission to retain
and forgive (or bind and loose) sins. The Church as a whole received
the gift of the Holy Spirit. The sinner has offended the whole people
of God and must be reconciled to them if he wishes to live again in
the Holy Spirit of God.[72]

---

[70] Hubbard, Jr. *St Augustine's Notion of Penance and Reconciliation with the
Church*, 65
[71] Ibid., 68
[72] Ibid., 71

'Lazarus, come forth' were spoken. And
he came forth from the tomb, his hands
and feet bound with bandages. The Lord summons the dead man to
come forth from
the tomb, and the sinner, whose heart
has been touched, io come forth by his confession of sin. But he is still
bound a little (parum). And so the Lord, after Lazarus had
come out of the tomb, said to his disciples (to whom he had
already said, 'whatsoever you loose on earth, shall be loosed
also in heaven'): 'loose him and let him go.' Lazarus is sum-
moned forth by him and loosed by his disciples. (Serm. 295, 2)
Lazarus is compared with a sinner. Both are dead until the grace of
Christ calls out to them. Yet even after 'coming
forth,' both are 'bound.' As the disciples loosed Lazarus
from his bandages, they must loose the sinner from his guilt.
Interestingly enough, this passage occurs almost immediately after
the excerpt from the same Sermon quoted on pp. 72–73 above . There
Augustine had shown that the entire Church possessed radically the
power of binding and loosing sinners:
Has enim claves non homo unus, sed unitas accepit Ecclesiae.
Here he indicates that the grace of God initiates the process
of repentance and forgiveness.[73]

It should be mentioned in passing that Augustine places considerable
emphasis in the Lazarus parallel on the private confession of sins to
the bishop. Through this action the sinner
'comes forth' from the tomb even though he is still bound. It
is the first step in the sinner's return to peace with the Church and
thereby with God.[74]

---

73 Ibid., 76
74 Ibid., 79

Satisfaction for sin must be made to the Church as well as to God. Consequently, the bishops are empowered to assign periods of penance depending upon the gravity of the sin. The idea of sin as an offense against the people of God was mentioned in connection with our evaluation of the penitential liturgy in Augustine's time. Here the Bishop of Hippo clearly states the idea. He then gives its theological basis: the Church has received the Holy Spirit as her source of the Christ- life only in the Spirit and hence in the Church are sins forgiven. The quotation is really a summary of Augustine's whole thought on penance and reconciliation with the Church.[75]

---

[75] Ibid., 80

Then the guy appeared again and said something to the effect that the previous should be revisited under the rubric of the opening, non-Hubbard, note; the one from him about the nature and usefulness of gold. And that it should be understood that the Hubbard quotes 'aid one in understanding the thought of Augustine in relation to the Sacrament of Reconciliation, specifically, which is one of the main points of disputation that resulted in the Donatist schism and against which Augustine strove to overcome and heal the Church. So, let's look at this again.'

The film played, again, on repeat, showing the whole sequence, again, and again and again
17 times.

Then he appeared for what he said was 'my penultimate time to stand before you.'
He said similar *look and listen and memorize and commit to memory long-term loop style* effort was to be given in seeing how '100% Catholic Saint Augustine was and is. Consider these quotes, the heading topic of which will be listed at the top of the successive pages and look and see.'

The film became to pop, whirr, and fizz forward once again.

The Holy Eucharist

76

What you see is the bread and the chalice; that is what your own eyes report to you. But what your faith obliges you to accept is that the bread is the body of Christ and the chalice is the blood of Christ. This has been said very briefly, which may perhaps be sufficient for faith; yet faith does not desire instruction.

We do not sin when we adore Christ in the Eucharist; we do sin when we do not adore Christ in the Eucharist.

Christ held Himself in His hands when He gave His Body to His disciples saying: 'This is My Body.' No one partakes of this Flesh before he has adored it.

I had promised those of you who have just been baptized a sermon to explain the sacrament of the Lord's table, which you can see right now, and which you shared in last night. You ought to know what you have received, what you are about to receive, what you ought to receive every day. That bread which you can see on the altar, sanctified by the word of God, is the body of Christ. That cup, or rather what the cup contains, sanctified by the word of God, is the blood of Christ.

---

76 For the following please see: St. Augustine, *Sermons* (AD 411); *Missionaries of the Blessed Sacrament* 'St. Augustine of Hippo, Bishop, Doctor of the Church, N. Africa (354–430), Feast Day, August 28'; 'An Easter Sermon of Saint Augustine to Newly Baptized Catholics,' sourced at *The American Catholic, Politics and Culture from a Catholic Perspective*, theamericancatholic.com; McShaunessaey, *The Interconnected Web-Currents of Saint Augustine of Hippo's Thought*, 400–401.

The Blessed Virgin Mary

77

[78]Not the visible sun, but the invisible Creator of the sun has consecrated this day on which the Virgin, a true but inviolate Mother, gave birth to Him who became visible for our sake and by whom she herself was created. A virgin conceives, yet remains a virgin: a virgin is heavy with child; a virgin brings forth her child, yet she is always a virgin. **Why are you amazed at this, O man? It was fitting for God to be born thus when He deigned to become man.**

He knew His mother in predestination, even before He was born of her; even before, as God, He created her of whom, as man, He was to be created, He knew her as His mother. He chose the Mother he had created; he created the Mother he had chosen.

Having excepted the Holy Virgin Mary, concerning whom, on account of the honor of the Lord, I wish to have absolutely no question when treating of sins—for how do we know what abundance of grace for the total over-coming of sin was conferred upon her, who merited to conceive and bear him in whom there was no sin?—so, I say, with the exception of the Virgin, if we could have gathered together all those holy men and women, when they were living here, and had asked them whether they were without sin, what do we suppose would have been

---

77 For the following please see: St. Augustine, *Sermons* (186,1), (Trac. In Iohanem 8,9), *Sermons* (69,3); St. Augustine, *Nature and Grace*; McShaunessaey, *The Interconnected Web-Currents of Saint Augustine of Hippo's Thought*, 401–403.

78 (In a homily on Christmas, he affirmed).... →

their answer?

Confession

79

Next, the Lord's Prayer is said which you have already received and recited. Why is it said before receiving the Body and Blood of Christ? Because of our human frailty perhaps our minds imagined something which is not becoming, our eyes saw something which was not decent, our ears heard something exaggeratedly which was not fitting. If perhaps such things have been kept in because of temptation and the fragility of human life, they are washed away by the Lord's Prayer at the moment we say, 'Forgive us our trespasses' so that we can safely approach the sacrament.

---

79 For the following please see: St. Augustine, (*Sermon 272/Ad Infantes, de Sacramento*, volume XXXVIII) McShaunessaey, *The Interconnected Web-Currents of Saint Augustine of Hippo's Thought*, 404–405.

The Character of the Church

80

No one can have God as his Father who does not have the Church as his mother.[81]

I would not believe in the Gospel, if the authority of the Catholic Church did not bid me to do so.

The custom of Mother Church in baptizing infants is certainly not to be scorned, nor is it to be regarded in any way as superfluous, nor is it to be believed that its tradition is anything except apostolic.

Wicked sons do not have the Holy Ghost in the same way as do beloved sons, and yet they do have Baptism. So, too, heretics do not have the Church as Catholics have, even though they have Baptism.

There is nothing more serious than the sacrilege of schism because there is no just cause for severing the unity of the Church.

---

[80] For the following please see: St. Augustine, 'Against the Fundamental Epistle of Manichaeus;' St. Augustine, 'On Baptism, Against the Donatists (Book 1):' Marcus Grodi, 'The Early Church Fathers I Never Saw as a Protestant Pastor,' *Coming Home Network International*, online citation: https://chnetwork.org/2012/04/24/the-early-church-fathers-i-never-saw-by-marcus-grodi/; McShaunessaey, *The Interconnected Web-Currents of Saint Augustine of Hippo's Thought*, 406–411.

[81] Father LeBron seems to be confusing/mix-matching Church Fathers here as, according to scholars, this quote was actually said by Saint Cyprian (AD 200–258), Bishop and Martyr of Carthage. Please see: https://christianhistoryinstitute.org/study/module/cyprian and/or/especially St. Cyprian's treatise 'On the Unity of the Church' https://www.newadvent.org/fathers/050701.htm

The man then appeared a final time, now smoking a cigarette, holding a glass of whiskey in his other hand. 'I'm going to play a final slide seven times,' he said, 'just so you, they, he, she, and all people, I mean everyone everywhere, gets it... got it? But note: the first six slides will go on in succession. Before the seventh there will be 5 BLANK PAGES just to prep your often blank mind to really get it, got it?'

He extinguished his cigarette in the glass of whiskey, threw it off a side wall, the smash of it pyrotechnically impressive, and walked away.

Pop, whirr,

fizz

forward

SAINT AUGUSTINE WAS NOT
A PROTESTANT.
HE'S ONE OF OURS.
KICK ROCKS, PUNCH WALLS.

HE'S CATHOLIC.

SAINT AUGUSTINE WAS NOT
A PROTESTANT.
  HE'S ONE OF OURS.
  KICK ROCKS, PUNCH WALLS.

  HE'S CATHOLIC.

SAINT AUGUSTINE WAS NOT
A PROTESTANT.
   HE'S ONE OF OURS.
   KICK ROCKS, PUNCH WALLS.

   HE'S CATHOLIC.

SAINT AUGUSTINE WAS NOT
A PROTESTANT.
HE'S ONE OF OURS.
KICK ROCKS, PUNCH WALLS.

HE'S CATHOLIC.

SAINT AUGUSTINE WAS NOT
A PROTESTANT.
HE'S ONE OF OURS.
KICK ROCKS, PUNCH WALLS.

HE'S CATHOLIC.

SAINT AUGUSTINE WAS NOT
A PROTESTANT.
   HE'S ONE OF OURS.
   KICK ROCKS, PUNCH WALLS.

   HE'S CATHOLIC.

SAINT AUGUSTINE WAS NOT
A PROTESTANT.
HE'S ONE OF OURS.
KICK ROCKS, PUNCH WALLS.

HE'S CATHOLIC.

The film went back to static. Then back to black. This
time, for
good.

Not a moment too soon for the three of them turn at
the same time to see the kn-   -ock
                    at t-
                    -he door.

They've arrived, the four
                    horseman.
            This, yes, only except for the fact that
there are no horses, only four guys, and they've come as if
snowshoeing. The snowshoes still cramped onto their feet,
the four of them holding a total of eight poles, naturally
well geared up, all of them, wearing what looks to be
very hearty and sturdy winter coats and hats and gloves
and each of them has a backpack and so *it's got to be them,
right?*, Mark thinks.

They knock again.

Father LeBron turns off the projector and opens the door. A great gust of cold, no, freezing air shoots in and hits them directly in the face. Mark winces. Anna puts out her cheeks all the more, in the *yes, please, give me some more of that*, fashion. The four guys—they look to be about the same size: medium build, height ranging anywhere from 5'7 to 5'10—did this, rather this is what happened *to them*, from first foot into the door, and this is the literal retelling of the scene, no embellishments, just the facts, as it was, as it is, nothing more or less.

Imagine:
it's low A baseball somewhere in the summer of 1882, somewhere in Iowa, not far from what was then called Iowa College, and the Field of Dreams this is here not, it is yet not, (I don't even know if they had moved the mound back to the correct 60'6" distance[82]), and if the batter could work a count full to a 3-2 numeration[83], another ball or another strike ending the plate appearance slash at bat, depending on formers and latters, and but so but on June 17, 1882, because it is June 17, 1882, and baseball in Iowa and Iowans know that was the date of the Great Summer Cyclone of 1882[84] and so but so imagine someone but so really but imagine someone announcing

---

[82] No, had not yet gone to 60'6". That happened eleven years later in 1893.

[83] No, because 4 balls, 3 strikes maximums making a full count what we all know a full count is—3 and 2—was established in 1889.

[84] Grinnell College (IA), 'Destruction and Rebirth: The Cyclone of 1882 Transcript,' https://www.grinnell.edu/about/leadership/offices-services/communications/podcast/all-things-grinnell/cyclone/transcript

this game—aha, yes, once more: pre television and pre even radio, for diehard fans know the first radio game broadcast would not come until almost four decades later: Pirates vs. Phillies on August the 5th of 1921; now that's only 3 years after the Great War, don't you know; so just imagine, just imagine it any way you would like—that someone announcing this game is like, 'The count is 2–1, folks, Anderson works from the stretch, checking the runners at second and third. 2 outs, bottom of the sixth and . . . excuse me, wait, yes, yes that is a tornado, a large tornado approaching with considerable speed and it looks like it's on a direct path towards the left center field wall!.' So, yes, as it was, as it is, just the score, just the

facts.
The,

(. . . . . this, rather this is what happened *to them* . . . . first foot into the
door →)

Each one of these four, well outfitted for the winter conditions of the Old Moscow Pullman Highway Four Horseman, walked in from the outside, made a start to remove something, a hat, a glove, but, having each one of them, and in quick succession like a domino hits a domino keeps on hitting all of dominoes, dominoes, dominoes until London Bridge is Falling Down,[85] Falling Down, Falling Down, London I mean Domino Bridge is falling down, my fair lady, looked over at Anna, caught a glimpse, that's all it takes, and went through a very rapid mental process of keywords

---

[85] The famous nursery rhyme is said to have been composed sometime in the 1740s but it may prove to have an even earlier, if murky, origin date of the late Middle Ages.

'woman,'
'wow,'
'beautiful,'
'the most,'
'ever'

before passing out, passing out cold.

The Heyburn Front Desk Effect had struck yet again.

It took more than half an hour to get all four of them revived and into sitting positions on couches and chairs.

'Look,' Father Lebron says, showing them a magazine that had featured Anna in her heyday. It was photo shoot she had done in the Gulf of Mexico on an oil rig. It was considered her 'Iconic shoot.' 'Look,' he says again, flipping back and forth through the photos. 'This is Anna Davenport. She's here. You idiots have to deal with that. Can you handle this type of beauty? Look,' showing them all the photos, again and again. It must have been working for the four guys seemed to be progressing from first look blacked out to now *I'm looking, like I'm looking at a Da Vinci painting, or a Michelangelo sculpture, but appreciating it, conscious.* 'You guys understand? She's here. You have to deal with that. Because we've got serious things to get down to. Are you okay, are you ready to look at her again in real life?'

The four men nod. Anna comes back into the room.
This time only one of them faints. He gets the Gulf Coast
oil rig treatment again. This time, what is meant is afterwards, after coming to, again, he's okay, his legs get a little
shaky, laying eyes on her a third time, but he does not
pass out. Mark, seeing all this, having been witness to
this entire scene, feels a mixture of embarrassment and
pride. The former for them, these four guys, haha, four
horsemen, my ass, you don't get a title like that if you
faint in the presence of a pretty woman. But then—and
here came the pride. Mark had been working on this,
pride, it was usually at the top of his 'Bless me Father
for I have sinned it has been six weeks…' list—but
then, again, then the pride that I'm nothing like these
tools, these B-team third stringers, horseMEN haha,
yeah, right
because

yeah, I walked up to Gulf Coast Anna first day, first date
in the restaurant and told her what's up. Let her know, yo.

And: hey.

And: hey, girl.

And: Girl, look. Girl, what up.

Also: this is me, that's you, now it's gonna be we,
going forward. That's how it's gonna be,
done.

Clear your books,   298
Every guy who thought with you
had a shot, so cooked.   300
They looked
for love
But your number I had already booked,
Love.
My name's Mark I got the right stuff
Other dudes clowns, they just ain't buff
When it comes to biceps, triceps, or the face   307
My photo always showing up in the right place
Perennial front page, the competition I displace
Compared to me all women a deep distaste
for every other man.   311
I'm the only man with the plan. Bam, bam, bam,
That's the sound of bazookas shooting stacks of money. I've got so
much money,
honey. I've—   314

'Mark, Mark!' Father LeBron says, the second time along with a pretty forceful smack across the face. Ouch. No, really, it was, it felt like, like,

ow.

'What was that for?' Mark says, rubbing his cheek.

'What is it with you two?' Father LeBron says. 'First, it's Anna. Zoning out for hours. Now you, the same. You know, I said your name   seven

seven

seven

seven

seven

seven

seven

times.

I tried to get your attention seven

seven

seven

seven

seven

seven

seven

times.

If you need a physical alarm clock, cool, no worries. But can we please get on task? Between the two of you daydreamers, and guests unable to stay conscious. . . . son of an expletive

be— eeeeeeeeeeeeeeeeeeeeeeeeeee
eeeeeeeeeeeeeeeeeeeeeeeeeeee eeeeeeeeeeeeeeeeeeeeeeeeeeee
eeeeeeeeeeeeeeeeeeeeeeeeeeee eeeeeeeeeeeeeeeeeeeeeeeeeeee
eeeeeeeeeeeeeeeeeeeeeeeeeeee eeeeeeeeeeeeeeeeeeeeeeeeeeee
eeeeeeeeeeeeeeeeeeeeeeeeeeee eeeeeeeeeeeeeeeeeeeeeeeeeeee
eeeeeeeeeeeeeeeeeeeeeeeeeeee eeeeeeeeeeeeeeeeeeeeeeeeeeee
eeeeeeeeeeeeeeeeeeeeeeeeeeee eeeeeeeeeeeeeeeeeeeeeeeeeeee
eeeeeeeeeeeeeeeeeeeeeeeeeeee eeeeeeeeeeeeeeeeeeeeeeeeeeee
eeeeeeeeeeeeeeeeeeeeeeeeeeee eeeeeeeeeeeeeeeeeeeeeeeeeeee
eeeeeeeeeeeeeeeeeeeeeeeeeeee eeeeeeeeeeeeeeeeeeeeeeeeeeee
eeeeeeeeeeeeeeeeeeeeeeeeeeee eeeeeeeeeeeeeeeeeeeeeeeeeeee
eeeeeeeeeeeeeeeeeeeeeeeeeeee eeeeeeeeeeeeeeeeeeeeeeeeeeee
eeeeeeeeeeeeeeeeeeeeeeeeeeee eeeeeeeeeeeeeeeeeeeeeeeeeeee
eeeeeeeeeeeeeeeeeeeeeeeeeeee eeeeeeeeeeeeeeeeeeeeeeeeeeee
eeeeeeeeeeeeeeeeeeeeeeeeeeee eeeeeeeeeeeeeeeeeeeeeeeeeeee
eeeeeeeeeeeeeeeeeeeeeeeeeeee eeeeeeeeeeeeeeeeeeeeeeeeeeee
eeeeeeeeeeeeeeeeeeeeeeeeeeee eeeeeeeeeeeeeeeeeeeeeeeeeeee
eeeeeeeeeeeeeeeeeeeeeeeeeeee eeeeeeeeeeeeeeeeeeeeeeeeeeee
eeeeeeeeeeeeeeeeeeeeeeeeeeee eeeeeeeeeeeeeeeeeeeeeeeeeeee
eeeeeeeeeeeeeeeeeeeeeeeeeeee eeeeeeeeeeeeeeeeeeeeeeeeeeee
eeeeeeeeeeeeeeeeeeeeeeeeeeee eeeeeeeeeeeeeeeeeeeeeeeeeeee
eeeeeeeeeeeeeeeeeeeeeeeeeeee eeeeeeeeeeeeeeeeeeeeeeeeeeee
eeeeeeeeeeeeeeeeeeeeeeeeeeee eeeeeeeeeeeeeeeeeeeeeeeeeeee
eeeeeeeeeeeeeeeeeeeeeeeeeeee eeeeeeeeeeeeeeeeeeeeeeeeeeee
eeeeeeeeeeeeeeeeeeeeeeeeeeee eeeeeeeeeeeeeeeeeeeeeeeeeeee
eeeeeeeeeeeeeeeeeeeeeeeeeeee eeeeeeeeeeeeeeeeeeeeeeeeeeee
eeeeeeeeeeeeeeeeeeeeeeeeeeee eeeeeeeeeeeeeeeeeeeeeeeeeeee
eeeeeeeeeeeeeeeeeeeeeeeeeeee eeeeeeeeeeeeeeeeeeeeeeeeeeee
eeeeeeeeeeeeeeeeeeeeeeeeeeee eeeeeeeeeeeeeeeeeeeeeeeeeeee
eeeeeeeeeeeeeeeeeeeeeeeeeeee eeeeeeeeeeeeeeeeeeeeeeeeeeee
eeeeeeeeeeeeeeeeeeeeeeeeeeee eeeeeeeeeeeeeeeeeeeeeeeeeeee
eeeeeeeeeeeeeeeeeeeeeeeeeeee eeeeeeeeeeeeeeeeeeeeeeeeeeee
eeeeeeeeeeeeeeeeeeeeeeeeeeee eeeeeeeeeeeeeeeeeeeeeeeeeeee
eeeeeeeeeeeeeeeeeeeeeeeeeeee eeeeeeeeeeeeeeeeeeeeeeeeeeee
eeeeeeeeeeeeeeeeeeeeeeeeeee— p.

Am I the only fully functioning person in this whole cohort? Like you said,' pointing at Mark, 'I'm "95 years old." I'm the guy who should be taking naps and being handed a warm cup of tea from a nice nurse in her late 20s with a great, truly great, almost dental hygienist level, beautiful smile—the kind of smile that will make a single man who just has his teeth cleaned respond to her saying: "okay, that just about does it, spit in that cup right there, and watch your head as I bring the seat back up. Would you like a new toothbrush and some floss in your Dental Hygiene goodie bag?" "No, thank you. Can I have your number though? Would you like to get a cup of coffee sometime?"—I'm the one here who should be zoning out, dozing off mid-thought into dreamlands replete with chess championships with my friends, Rottweilers frolicking in wild flowered covered hills, pool party at noon, I'm already in my trunks, bridge?, check, pinochle?, you already know Thelma and Stella are running that table daily at 2:45 PM; watching reruns of *Mary Tyler Moore* and *The Brady Bunch* after dinner at 4pm. But you two,' pointing again at Mark, but this time at Anna in equal measure, 'you just can't seem to stay on task. Get it together, okay? Can we please get this whole deal back on the tracks and moving once more? Someone once commenting on how the Buffalo Bills 100% got that fourth quarter fourth and 1 against the Kansas City Chiefs in the 2025 AFC Championship because their QB, Josh Allen, who had gained the yardage on a QB sneak, is, quote, built like a runaway freight train, meaning by that there is no way you stopped him on that play, basically read my mind perfectly: please, can we, please make this session 5 a runaway train where, even if we wanted to stop it, we could not, ensuring that we will, finally and mercifully, finish this, this second to last session.'

'That hurt real bad,' Mark says, still rubbing his face.

'Stop being such a pansy, such a little b—

'It hurt, man!' Mark protests, 'you hit me with YOUR hand.... YOU have an almost thousand pound deadlift. You hit me with a hand that has grip strength like that. I thought, I thought that a boxer had just right hooked me, that slap.'

'Are you ready or not?' the priest says. 'Last time I'm asking or we're shutting down this fifth session. If no, not ready, and if shut down yes, I'm going to go out to the gym and do light weight, 4, 500 pounds, but something like 80 sets, 75 reps per set. And I'll blast that awful music where the guys just flip out and yell stuff that makes no sense as loud as possible into the microphone as loud as possible. Double, they're as loud as can be, I'll play it as loud as the stereo will allow. I promise, I'll break the dial turning it right as forcefully as I can to get it as loud as possible! Don't make me do it. I promise I will, don't make me.'

'Why don't you play hip hop when you lift?' Mark asks. 'Isn't that better?'

'Hip hop?' Father LeBron asks.

'Yeah, you know,' Mark says, proceeding to demonstrate, free styling for only about ten seconds. It's enough to get Anna dancing again, just like on the airplane.

Anna is such a good dancer it's truly hard to explain. Suffice to say: the greatest female model of all time might have missed her calling as a dancer.

'So...what are we doing?' Father Lebron says.

'Let's continue the fifth sessions, Father,' Anna says, eagerly. Emphasis on the word *eager*. It's perfectly done, her response. That pilot, rather the FAA guy, who thought she was a movie star, and was then corrected by John Anderson, pilot, that, not a movie star but a model, maybe was on to something. So perhaps two different life callings missed (?) and yet what a landing still. Her response, just so well done. For it was like she had really said, 'now, Father, dearest, I do believe, and with every fiber of my heart, that yes, that it would be excellent, quite swell even, if you would continue. Oh, please, Father, we hang on thy every word.'

Mark loved it too.

His thoughts right now are basically, Anna,

Anna,

Anna, Anna, Anna.... Anna.

Anna.

Anna.

Father Lebron, as is becoming standard practice, is pacified and encouraged by Anna.

The four horseman are sitting on the couch. Each one of them alert.

So maybe this fifth session can then be seen through to the finish?

'What are your names?' Father LeBron asks the four horsemen.

'Matthew,' the first one says.

'Mark,' the next one right next to him says.

The next two follow in, if one were to be paying attention, the anticipated order.

'Luke.'

'John.'

'No, no, no,' Father LeBron says. 'No. No.'

The four look at him with blank stares.

'While you're here, you'll go by Matty, Marky, Lukey, and Johnny.'

Luke does not like this and makes a start to protest.

'Are any of you Catholic?' Father LeBron asks.

They all, and practically at the same time, shake their head side to side.

No.

'So what are you?'

They answer in the same order they had introduced themselves.

'Christian. Non-denominational.'

'Christian. Um . . . Baptist, I think. No, wait, Presby-, no, Methodist. That's my family history. Yeah. Um . . . yeah, yep.'

'LDS. Mormon. Latter Day Saints.'

'Just Christian.'

'Lukey,' Father LeBron says. 'You're Mormon?'

'Yeah.'

'Dude, you have no idea what God has planned for the Mormons.'

'No, I, I think I do. I mean Heavenly Father—

'You have no idea,' Father LeBron reiterates.

'He can read souls,' Anna says.

'What?' Luke asks.

'He can see beyond normal things,' Mark says. Mark the Model says, it should be specified, not Mark the Horseman.

Mark the one who told Gulf Coast Anna what was up, girl, what up. 'God has blessed him with . . . he just knows things, man. It is what it is.'

'What is?' Luke says.

'God has huge, huge plans for the Mormons, Lukey,' Father LeBron says. 'I'm talking about 1531 hill of Tepeyac style. I'm talking about millions and millions of Aztecs doing very, very big bad stuff but then, in one instant, God sends Nuestra Senora and, just about overnight, all these formerly bad guys convert to the one true Faith and Mexico is born and, *vamonos.* Just think:

Our Lady of the Salt Lake Valley.

Get hyped, Lukey, just imagine, all your people, good people, some of the best people in terms of morals and downhome values and all that but, now, but this, going door to door all over the world for the capital T truth my friend. I'm saying, let's go.'

'Look,' Luke says, 'Mister, um, Father, Father Le—... is, is your name actually LeBron? Father LeBron?'

'Yes, sir,' Father Lebron says. 'An old Irish name very popular in County Cork.'

'Really?'

'No. But, yes, that is my actual name.'

'Okay. Father Lebron, can you please call us by our proper names and not these infantilizing, stupid, insulting diminutives?'

'No.'

'...'

'No, sorry.'

'Why?'

'Okay, look. You and me, one on one, right now. First one to three, make it take it.'

'What?'

'You heard me. You win, I call you Matthew, Mark, et cetera. But you lose, you ride and die with the names I gave you for as long as you're here.'

The whole group heads out to the basketball hoop affixed to what looks like a 19th century telegraph pole that is basically right there in the middle of the outdoor weight room. They shoot for ball. Guests go first and good for Father LeBron for, as Mark the model knows, he's really, really bad at the fundamentals of the game, shooting at the top of the list. But, on the other hand, Mark the model does not think Luke the Mormon Horseman is anywhere near ready for the type of athleticism the old priest has. It's going to come down to this opening shot for ball. If Luke makes it, triple win. His ball, he's a good shot so maybe he can make three more, and, he doesn't have to play defense against Father LeBron.

Luke misses.

Father LeBron drives past him on the opening possession and dunks, two handed. Luke looks genuinely surprised. But of course. Luke tries to play better D next possession but to no avail. Father LeBron backs him down into the paint, pumps left, Luke bites, then spins right and two hands another dunk. 2–0, priest. On possession three Father LeBron makes known, with actions, not words, that he's done playing around and he really wants to wrap up this spiritual advising session number 5. He takes one step to the right and then takes off, *he takes off*, from behind the foul line and throws down a massive windmill dunk to finish off his opponent, finishing the game.

'Matty, Marky, Lukey, and Johnny,' he says. 'Ha. You all ready to begin?'

Matthew answers right away. 'Yes. But, wait, we, the four of us, have information for Mark and Anna of the highest importance.'

'Not now,' Father LeBron says. 'Just wait.'

'Just wait?' Mark the model asks. 'Just wait? You've been flipping out the whole time. *Let's go, oh, c'mon, boo hoo,* and all that. You just threw a tantrum before threatening to do over a thousand total deadlift reps if we didn't get on with it and now you're saying slow down?'

'I didn't say slow down. I said, no. I said: wait. And, wait, yeah, because our friends just showed up and we gotta recap this session for them. Then they can say what they came to say.'

Father LeBron puts the Rod Serling guy back on.

5 minutes[86] from completion ([87]) one of the horsemen, Luke, jumps in, hands waving, and says, rather, exclaims,

'Stop. Please. Please don't continue. We've heard enough. Right, guys?'

Mark and Matthew and John all nod in unison.

'We want to become Catholic,' John says.

'Really?' Father LeBron asks.

'Yes,' Mark says.

'All of you?'

'All of us,' Matthew replies. 'Luke, are you in?'

'Am I in? I started this interruption for precisely this reason. Yeah, I'm in.'

Anna looks at Mark ([88]) and smiles.

'Well, then,' Father LeBron says. 'I hereby do declare: you are henceforth and forever more to be called, and only referred to, as Matthew, Mark, Luke, and John. Weighty names worthy of the Evangelical predecessors from which they stem.'

'Can we do it now?' Mark the Horseman asks.

'What?' Father LeBron asks.

'Become Catholic.'

'Wait. Yes, we'll start the process immediately. I'll be happy to take the four of you on as advisees. We'll begin what they call RCIA right away. The Rite of Christian

---

[86] Counted down would be like: 5:00, 4:59, 4:58, 4:57, 4:56... (4 minutes later)... 0:56, 0:55, 0:54, 0:53, 0:52, 0:51... (49 seconds later)... 0:02, 0:01, 0:00.

[87] on run 1 of 17 total.

[88] her husband.

Initiation for Adults. You won't be able to formally enter the Church yet, or partake of her sacraments, but soon, the next Easter, yes. We'll start right away. God bless you. May God bless the four of you, oh noble and valorous horsemen! Now, what have you come to tell the King and Queen of Modeling? You had an urgent message, right?'

John, who to this point had not said too much, stands up and steps up, to the plate as it were, wasting no time, right to the point.

'Yes. I have a message from the President of the United States for Mark and Anna. This is the whole reason for us coming here, across this ice, this now fjord-like road as far as the eye can see. Aliens have flooded and hardened the Old Moscow Pullman Highway. It is a simultaneous demonstration of their power, being far more technologically advanced than we are, and a condition of their proposal. Mark and Anna have forty hours—actually 40 hours and ten minutes and eleven seconds from this very moment—to decide whether they accept or reject the aliens' terms.[89] The proposal is as follows: a two-person, husband and wife, modeling show. One show, a few hours tops, but on the moon. They aliens will provide to and from transportation. If Mark and Anna accept and do it, the aliens will melt the ice, stop all this nonsense,' pointing outside, 'and move on to another galaxy. If they say no, it's thousands of lasers that are currently aimed at

Planet Earth having their trigger, their ON button, their, well you get it; pushed or pressed or "fired," call it what you want to call it. One of these lasers can blow up the world. But they're going to fire them all if you guys,' gesturing toward Mark and Anna, 'say no. Still, the president said the aliens told him: *it's their choice*. It's like that old super, super simultaneously catchy and obnoxious

---

[89] Terms, period, not Terms & Conditions, although Conditions, Cause, and Effect are all here present in ample measure.

money commercial: "it's your money, use it when you need it."[90] Your choice, Mark and Anna, use it how and when you need it. But look, you do need to decide. The president said they, the aliens, said this to him—all these things about choices and free will—because according to him, the president, they, the aliens, are huge fans of Saint Augustine of Hippo. They're all about free will. You have to deal with the consequences of the free choices you make, but you are free. That's what the president told me the aliens told him. The aliens also told the president their favorite book by Saint Augustine is *83 Different Questions,* and that you'll find all you want to about this free will stuff in question 24.[91] He also told me the aliens told him they love Augustine's just war theory. If Mark and Anna refuse to do the fashion show they are confident they will be justified in blowing up Planet Earth.'

---

[90] J. G. Wentworth.

[91] Q. 24. —Do Sin and Conduct Result from a Free Choice of the Will? A '...this good we also call Divine Providence. Therefore nothing happens in the world by chance. This having been established, it seems to follow that whatever is done in the world is done partly by divine agency and partly by our will. For God is by far incomparably better and more just than any man, no matter how good and just. And the just ruler and governor of all things allows no punishment to be inflicted undeservedly on anyone, nor any reward to be given undeservedly to anyone. That which merits punishment is sin, and that which merits reward is right conduct. And neither sin nor right conduct can be justly charged to anyone who has done nothing of his own will. Accordingly sin and right conduct result from a free choice of the will.' The Fathers of the Church, Saint Augustine, *83 Different Questions* (trans. David L. Mosher, Washington, D. C.: Catholic University of America Press, 1977), 50–51.

6

On Time and the Eternal Now

'40 hours,' Father LeBron says. 'The Forty Hours Eucharist Devotion. Christ's forty days in the Desert, the first Lent. The Great Flood: Forty Days and Forty Nights.'

'We're obviously going to do it, right?' Mark asks.

'Obviously,' Anna says, exhaling, cupping a cup of coffee, putting it to her lips for a sip then a second. The four horsemen are gone. That was part of the deal too, they said. *We're but the messengers,* they said, further explaining that the president and the aliens had entrusted them with the delivery of the conditions, the proposal, but that they were to leave immediately afterwards.

And so they had.

They resolved to come back to the secret restaurant on the Old Moscow Pullman Highway for their own spiritual advising, RCIA, with Father LeBron as soon as 'all this was over.' Such was their confidence in Mark the Model and his wife, Gulf Coast Anna of the Oil Rig. They were going to deliver. They had not—not until this very moment now, a literal few seconds ago—confirmed that they, Mark and Anna, were going to do this alien hosted, Grand Photo Shoot on the Moon, but still, the others, Father Lebron and the Four Horsemen, they believed in them; Mark and Anna.

So, the Four Horseman had said to Father Lebron:

'We'll be back.'

In that short period after the Horsemen had left, Father LeBron had some fun with the models. Mark,

he really had set himself up for it.

'So,' he had said to the priest. 'Aliens. They're, they're real?'

'Yep.'

Mark shook his head.

'They are. You know what Shakespeare said: There are more things in Heaven and Earth....

'But how do you know? Why, because some guys came across the ice and claimed the president sent them. This is so stupid, this sounds like-

'Because I am one,' Father LeBron said.

'...'

'Yep, I was born on Mars,' the priest said, 'went to college on Jupiter. Did a bunch of stuff I regret, you know, the internet is forever.'

'...'

'You know,' speaking to Mark, for Anna had just been listening and rather emotionless at/towards that. 'You really do live up to the idiot, brainless model stereotype. You got mad before, in an earlier session, about me saying how you go "full dumbass" often. Well, do you blame me?'

'Yeah, I blame you,' Mark said. 'I still don't know what's real here. Remember before, in that "full dumbass" exchange, when, at the end, you apologized because I was asking if this was the end of the world or not and you were saying me asking that was "full dumbass" but then because of these "Horsemen" like in the Book of Revelation you said, "oh, yeah, my bad;" so maybe again, your bad? Look, can you please drop all the bullshit and just speak plainly. Please. Is this real?'

'I do remember that,' Father LeBron said. 'We then got into that discussion about the University of Illinois and Littyville.'

'. . .'

'Yes,' the priest said. 'Let your yes mean yes, and your no mean no.[92] Here it is, plain: I'm not an alien, no shit, Sherlock, but, yes, aliens are real, those four guys have been sent by the president, yes, and their message is 100% as it appears to be on face value. You and Anna do the On the Moon photo shoot and you save the planet. Not like the beclowned environmental activists image they are or might. No, I'm mean, actually, you actually save the planet from extraterrestrial Armageddon. If you say no, and you can say no, remember Saint Augustine and free will, you have free will and free choices flowing therefrom, it all goes boom, boom, ba-ka-pow! So, that's it and that's all.'

And right at this moment, rather, two seconds or so after this moment, Father Lebron had said: '40 hours. The Forty Hours Eucharist Devotion. Christ's forty days in the Desert, the first Lent. The Great Flood: Forty Days and Forty Nights.'

And following this, Mark had said 'We're obviously going to do it, right?'

---

[92] Matthew 5:37.

And then Anna,

'Obviously.'

Then Mark says, NOW, to Anna and to Father Lebron:

None of us[93]   315
has one fixed home: we live in shady groves
and settle on soft riverbanks by Heyburn State Park or amidst lentil
fields on the
Old Moscow-Pullman Highway
where fresh streams flow. But if God's will
is for this, then let us climb however high and hard a hill
with all deliberate speed, not stopping, not hoping for an easy path.321
Soon speak, Father Lebron, and lead the way,
point out bright stars and new galaxies above. Let the aliens come and
with them
let us ascend
towards the Moon,   325
our destiny.
But in the deep golden fields of this auburn, purple valley, Father
Lebron, you now looking lost in thought, do thou study
the souls of your beloved Mark and Anna—and all the spiritual children to come,
four horsemen soon four Catholic
men, newly minted.
We are all of us, by God's grace, destined for the upper light.
The Moon first, but I speak still of that greater Kingdom
come. The Heavenly Jerusalem, Good Lord, I beg you aid me now cross
the meadow,
my wife and I stretching out our hands, willingly, to do Thy Will. Even
as the tears   335
run down Anna's face, these words I hear fall from her lips:
Has it come at last, our eternal destiny as models?
Matthew 25 talents to be put to a most noble purpose, our looks undefeated
despite the difficulty of the journey. Mark, my love,
what dangers battered you and us? What lands, what wide waters and
upper atmospheres have we traversed together, as husband and wife, to
make this lunar landing possible?   341
I look at your face—what beauty!—and you at mine, and I think back
to our first date, back,
before, to Corpus Christi, Texas, where many a happy day I passed
long ago and back,
to Miami, Florida, to our newly planted roots but back,
closer
to how it began and
now,
counting the moments,
I know my longing did not cheat me.   350

---

[93] Virgil, *The Aeneid* (trans. Mandelbaum), Book VI, 152–153.

'Okay, then,'
Father LeBron says.

'So it's settled.

But, before you depart we have two final items to attend to.
1. Prayers.
For do never forget, the Benedictines got it right so many
years ago,

ORA ET LABORA

"Prayer and Work." People,' Father LeBron says, 'will try to cross ocean, desert, and Antarctic shelf to find the key to it all but the Benedictines nailed it more than a millennium ago. It's all about prayer and work. You want to succeed in anything? Pray, first. Then: work. Work- grind your tail off the grindstone rise and grind. But first, pray. Also: fast. Also: give alms. But we'll save that for some other day.

Pray and Work.

So these final two items are
1. Prayer
And something like a 1.5 because 2, 2. Work, your work is to be done on the

Moon.

Okay, first, we'll pray and then
1.5 we'll review everything you guys learned. P. S. you passed—your spiritual advising sessions, spoiler alert, you passed with flying colors; turpentine honey gold most precisely.

1. 'Prayer:
Father Lebron tells them, 'number one of one. And
for the rest.... that number, 2, 3, 4, et cetera of one, one
being this first last item, 1. Prayer

1. every day, day or night, pray, at minimum,
-one Our Father
-one Hail Mary
-one Glory Be.

2. / 0. Just make the Sign of the Cross—itself a very powerful prayer—upon rising and retiring. And as another
0. Foundational thing: read the Bible every day, at least
fifteen minutes, Gospels first and above all, and maybe at
least a Psalm or two too.

3. Do the Divine Praises every day (and so they—Father
LeBron, Mark & Anna—did them out loud, together).

Blessed be God.
Blessed be his Holy Name.
Blessed be Jesus Christ, True God and True Man.
Blessed be the Name of Jesus.
Blessed be His most Sacred Heart.
Blessed be His most Precious Blood.
Blessed be Jesus in the most Holy Sacrament of the altar.
Blessed be the Holy Spirit, the Paraclete.
Blessed be the great Mother of God, Mary most holy.
Blessed be her holy and Immaculate Conception.
Blessed be her glorious Assumption.
Blessed be the name of Mary, Virgin and Mother.
Blessed be Saint Joseph, her most chaste Spouse.
Blessed be God in His Angels and in His Saints.

4. Pray the Rosary every day (and so they prayed it—Glorious Mysteries—out loud, together).

5. Pray the Divine Mercy Chaplet every day, especially at 3 o'clock (and so they prayed it, out loud, together).

6. Pray the Angelus every day, especially at noon, but if you want to go full French peasant, circa 1689, the year the King should have listened to Jesus and consecrated France to the Sacred Heart and so avoided what came one hundred years later, you can (and so they prayed it, out loud, together).

7. Pray the Litany of the Saints, the Litany of Loreto, and the Litany of St Joseph, at least once weekly (and so they prayed them, out loud, together, and in that order).

Litany of the Saints

Lord, have mercy on us. *Christ have mercy on us.*
Lord, have mercy on us. Christ, hear us, *Christ, graciously hear us.*
God, the Father of heaven, *Have mercy on us.*
God the Son, Redeemer of the world, *Have mercy on us.*
God, the Holy Spirit, Have mercy on us. Holy
Trinity, One God, *Have mercy on us.*

Holy Mary, *Pray for us.*
Holy Mother of God, *Pray for us.*
Holy Virgin of virgins, *Pray for us.*
Saint Michael, *Pray for us.*
Saint Gabriel, *Pray for us.*
Saint Raphael, *Pray for us.*
All ye holy angels and archangels, *Pray for us.*
All ye holy orders of blessed spirits, *Pray for us.*
Saint John the Baptist, *Pray for us.*
Saint Joseph, *Pray for us.*
All ye holy patriarchs and prophets. *Pray for us.*
Saint Peter, *Pray for us.*
Saint Paul, *Pray for us.*
Saint Andrew, *Pray for us.*
Saint James, *Pray for us.*
Saint John, *Pray for us.*
Saint Thomas, *Pray for us.*
Saint James, *Pray for us.*
Saint Philip, *Pray for us.*
Saint Bartholomew. *Pray for us.*
Saint Matthew, *Pray for us.*
Saint Simon, *Pray for us.*
Saint Thaddeus, *Pray for us.*
Saint Matthias, *Pray for us.*
Saint Barnabas, *Pray for us.*
Saint Luke, *Pray for us.*
Saint Mark, *Pray for us.*
All ye holy apostles and evangelists, *Pray for us.*
All ye holy disciples of our Lord. *Pray for us.*
All ye holy Innocents, *Pray for us.*
Saint Stephen, *Pray for us.*
Saint Lawrence, *Pray for us.*
Saint Vincent, *Pray for us.*
Saints Fabian and Sebastian, *Pray for us.*
Saints John and Paul, *Pray for us.*
Saints Cosmas and Damian, *Pray for us.*

Saints Gervase and Protase, *Pray for us.*
All ye holy martyrs, *Pray for us.*
Saint Sylvester, *Pray for us.*
Saint Gregory, *Pray for us.*
Saint Ambrose, *Pray for us.*
Saint Augustine. *Pray for us.*
Saint Jerome, *Pray for us.*
Saint Martin, *Pray for us.*
Saint Nicolas, *Pray for us.*
All ye holy bishops and confessors, *Pray for us.*
All ye holy doctors, *Pray for us.*
Saint Anthony, *Pray for us.*
Saint Benedict, *Pray for us.*
Saint Bernard, *Pray for us.*
Saint Dominic, *Pray for us.*
Saint Francis, Pray for us.
All ye holy priests and levites, *Pray for us.*
All ye holy monks and hermits. *Pray for us.*
Saint Mary Magdalen, *Pray for us.*
Saint Agatha, *Pray for us.*
Saint Lucy, *Pray for us.*
Saint Agnes, *Pray for us.*
Saint Cecily, *Pray for us.*
Saint Catherine, *Pray for us.*
Saint Anastasia, *Pray for us*
All ye holy virgins and widows, *Pray for us.*

All ye holy men and women, Saints of God, *Make intercession for us.*
Be merciful, *Spare us, O Lord.*
Be merciful, *Graciously hear us, O Lord.*

From all evil, *O Lord, deliver us.*
From all sin, *O Lord, deliver us.*
From Thy wrath, *O Lord, deliver us.*
From a sudden and unprovided death, *O Lord, deliver us.*
From the snares of the devil, *O Lord, deliver us.*
From anger, and hatred, and all ill will, *O Lord, deliver us.*
From the spirit of fornication, *O Lord, deliver us.*
From lightning and tempest, *O Lord, deliver us.*
From the scourge of earthquake. *O Lord, deliver us.*
From pestilence, famine and war, *O Lord, deliver us.*
From everlasting death, *O Lord, deliver us.*
Through the mystery of Thy holy Incarnation, *O Lord, deliver us.*
Through Thy coming, *O Lord, deliver us.*

Through Thy nativity, *O Lord, deliver us.*
Through Thy baptism and holy fasting, *O Lord, deliver us.*
Through Thy Cross and Passion, *O Lord, deliver us.*
Through Thy death and burial, *O Lord, deliver us.*
Through Thy holy Resurrection, *O Lord, deliver us.*
Through Thine admirable Ascension, *O Lord, deliver us.*
Through the coming of the Holy Spirit the Paraclete, *O Lord, deliver us.*
In the day of judgment, *O Lord, deliver us.*

We sinners, *We beseech Thee, hear us,*
That Thou wouldst spare us, *We beseech Thee, hear us.*
That Thou wouldst pardon us, *We beseech Thee, hear us.*
That Thou wouldst bring us to true penance, *We beseech Thee,
hear us.*
That Thou wouldst govern and preserve Thy holy Church *We beseech
Thee, hear us.,*
That Thou wouldst preserve our Aposto-lie Prelate, and all
ecclesiastical orders in holy religion, *We beseech Thee,
hear us,*
That Thou wouldst humble the enemies of Thy holy Church,
We beseech Thee, hear us.
That Thou wouldst give peace and true concord to Christian kings
and princes, *We beseech Thee, hear us.*
That Thou wouldst grant peace and unity to all Christian people, *We
beseech Thee, hear us.*
That Thou wouldst bring back to the unity of the Church all those
who have strayed away, and lead to the light of the Gospel all
unbelievers, *We beseech Thee, hear us.*
That Thou wouldst confirm and pres-erve us in Thy holy service, *We
beseech Thee, hear us.*
That Thou wouldst lift up our minds to heavenly desires, *We beseech
Thee, hear us.*
That Thou wouldst render eternal blessings to all our benefactors, *We
beseech Thee, hear us.*
That Thou wouldst deliver our souls, and the souls of our brethren,
relations and benefactors, from eternal damnation, *We beseech Thee,
hear us.*
That Thou wouldst give and preserve the fruit of the earth, *We beseech
Thee, hear us.*
That Thou wouldst give eternal rest to all the faithful departed, *We
beseech Thee, hear us.*
That Thou wouldst graciously hear us *We beseech Thee, hear us.* Son of
God, *We beseech Thee, hear us.*

Lamb of God, Who takest away the sins of the world, *Spare us, O Lord.*
Lamb of God, Who takest away the sins of the world, *Graciously hear us, O Lord.*
Lamb of God, Who takest away the sins of the world, *Have mercy on us.*

Christ hear us. *Christ, graciously hear us.*
Lord, have mercy on us. *Christ, have mercy on us.*
Lord, have mercy on us.

Litany of Loreto

Lord have mercy.
Christ have mercy.
Lord have mercy.
Christ hear us.
Christ graciously hear us.

God, the Father of heaven,
have mercy on us.

God the Son, Redeemer of the world,
God the Holy Spirit,
Holy Trinity, one God,

Holy Mary,
pray for us.
Holy Mother of God,
Holy Virgin of virgins,
Mother of Christ,
Mother of the Church,
Mother of Mercy,
Mother of divine grace,
Mother of Hope,
Mother most pure,
Mother most chaste,
Mother inviolate,
Mother undefiled,
Mother most amiable,
Mother admirable,
Mother of good counsel,
Mother of our Creator,
Mother of our Saviour,

Virgin most prudent,
Virgin most venerable,
Virgin most renowned,
Virgin most powerful,
Virgin most merciful,
Virgin most faithful,
Mirror of justice,
Seat of wisdom,
Cause of our joy,
Spiritual vessel,
Vessel of honour,
Singular vessel of devotion,
Mystical rose,
Tower of David,
Tower of ivory,
House of gold,
Ark of the covenant,
Gate of heaven,
Morning star,
Health of the sick,
Refuge of sinners,
Solace of Migrants,
Comfort of the afflicted,
Help of Christians,
Queen of Angels,
Queen of Patriarchs,
Queen of Prophets,
Queen of Apostles,
Queen of Martyrs,
Queen of Confessors,
Queen of Virgins,
Queen of all Saints,
Queen conceived without original sin,
Queen assumed into heaven,
Queen of the most holy Rosary,
Queen of families,
Queen of peace.

Lamb of God, who takes away the sins of the world,
spare us, O Lord.
Lamb of God, who takes away the sins of the world,
graciously hear us, O Lord.
Lamb of God, who takes away the sins of the world,
have mercy on us.

Pray for us, O holy Mother of God.
That we may be made worthy of the promises of Christ.

Let us pray.
Grant, we beseech thee,
O Lord God,
that we, your servants,
may enjoy perpetual health of mind and body;
and by the glorious intercession of the Blessed Mary, ever Virgin,
may be delivered from present sorrow,
and obtain eternal joy.
Through Christ our Lord.
Amen.

Litany of Saint Joseph

Lord, have mercy.
Christ, have mercy.
Lord, have mercy.
Christ, hear us.
Christ, graciously hear us.

God, the Father of Heaven, have mercy on us.
God the Son, Redeemer of the world, have mercy on us.
God the Holy Spirit, have mercy on us.
Holy Trinity, One God, have mercy on us.

Holy Mary, pray for us (after each line)
Saint Joseph,
Renowned offspring of David,
Light of Patriarchs,
Spouse of the Mother of God,
Chaste guardian of the Virgin,
Foster-father of the Son of God,
Diligent protector of Christ,
Head of the Holy Family,
Joseph most just,
Joseph most chaste,
Joseph most prudent,
Joseph most strong,
Joseph most obedient,
Joseph most faithful,

Mirror of patience,
Lover of poverty,
Model of artisans,
Glory of home life,
Guardian of virgins,
Pillar of families,
Solace of the wretched, Hope of the sick,
Patron of the dying,
Terror of demons,
Protector of Holy Church,

Lamb of God, who take away the sins of the world,
Spare us, O Lord.
Lamb of God, who take away the sins of the world,
Graciously hear us, O Lord.
Lamb of God, who take away the sins of the world,
Have mercy on us.

V. He made him the lord of His house:
R. And ruler of all His substance.

Let us pray.
O God, who in Thine unspeakable providence didst vouchsafe to choose
blessed Joseph to be the spouse of Thine own most holy Mother: grant,
we beseech Thee, that we may deserve to have him for our intercessor
in heaven, whom we reverence as our defender on earth: who livest
and reignest world without end. Amen.

8. If you want to go full monk, pray the Liturgy of the
Hours, the Divine Office. And remember that most perfect prayer therein, the double asking, nay, begging God
for help.

God, come to my assistance.
Lord, make haste to help me.
Glory be to the Father, and the Son, and the Holy Spirit.
Amen.

And finally—8/ 0.-foundational once again and a final time—attend, assist at, the Holy Sacrifice of the Mass. Sundays and Holy Days of obligation, yes, but daily, if you can. John 6—it's about that, full stop. Calvary, redemption, our salvation, it's about that. And 0., 0., 0., 0. level foundationals once more, do Eucharistic Adoration as often as you can. A daily Holy Hour? Wow. But even once per week, whenever you can, as much as you can.'

Mark and Anna asked Father Lebron if he would say Mass before they reviewed all the lessons and then left for the Moon.

He said *duh, that was the plan the whole time.*

What do you think of the Latin Mass v. Novus Ordo 'debates' in the Church, they asked him.

There's no debate, he said, be a faithful son and daughter of the Church. Nothing wrong with liking, even loving, the traditional Latin Mass. But since the Church, in her divinely protected wisdom, has said the Novus Ordo is the now ordinary form, the TLM, the extraordinary form, be accepting in that holy virtue of obedience. But still, doing this, nothing wrong about loving the TLM and maybe even hoping that in the future it returns to ordinary status.

What seems to be worst of all here, Mark opined, was the cultures that surrounded each 'debating faction.' The cringy and obnoxious 1970s guitar NO people and the cringy obnoxious women shouldn't vote or even speak I wish it was 1406 TLM people. It was the culture around each group that was the worst, Mark said. He continued that 'I wouldn't mind at all if all the Masses were TLM and give me that liturgy and the incense and the chiming bells and elaborate vestments DURING THE MASS but afterwards, just be normal. Please, please, please, please, please, please,

be normal.
Speak, normal.
Act, normal, all for the

GLORY OF GOD.

Father LeBron and Anna agreed wholeheartedly. They said so.

But so the Mass, Father Lebron then said, should I celebrate it in Latin?

Mark and Anna agreed wholeheartedly. They said so.

And so he did,

(excerpted notations pertaining there-to)

"Confitebor tibi in cithara, Deus, Deus meus: quare tristis es, anima mea, et quare conturbas me? Spera in Deo, quoniam adhuc confitebor illi, salutare vultus mei, et Deus meus. Gloria Patri, et Filio, et Spiritui Sancto. Sicut erat in principio, et nunc, et semper, et in sæcula sæculorum. Amen. Introibo ad altare Dei. Ad Deum lætificat juventutem meam. Adjutorium nostrum in nomine Domini. Qui fecit cælum et terram."

...

"Confiteor Deo omnipotenti, beatæ Mariæ semper Virgini ... quia peccavi nimis cogitatione, verbo et opere: mea culpa, mea culpa, mea maxima culpa ..."

...

"Misereaturi vestri omnipotens Deus, et dismissis peccatis vestris, perducat vos ad vitam æternam. Amen. Indulgentiam, absolutionem, et remissionem peccatorum nostrorum tribuat nobis omnipotens et misericors Domininus. Amen."

...

"Kyrie, eleison. *Kyrie, eleison.*
Kyrie, eleison. *Kyrie, eleison.*
Christe, eleison. *Christe, eleison.*
Kyrie, eleison. *Kyrie, eleison.*
Kyrie, eleison.

...

"Gloria in Excelsis Deo. Et in terra pax hominibus bonæ voluntatis. Ladumus te, Benedicimus te. Adoramus te, Glorificamus te. Gratias agumus tibi propter magnman glorium tuam. Domine Deus, Rex cælestis, Deus Pater omnipotens. Domine Fili unigenite, Jesu Christe. Domine Deus, Agnus Dei, Filius Patris. Qui tollis peccata mundi, miserere nobis. Qui tollis peccata mundi, suscipe depractionem nostram. Qui sedes ad dexteram Patris, miserere nobis. Quoniam tu solus Sanctus. Tu solus Dominus. Tu solus Altissimus, Jesu Christe. Cum Sancto Spiritu in gloria Dei Patris. Amen."

...

"Sequentia santci Evangelii secundum. Gloria tibi, Domine. Laus tibi, Christe. Per evangelica dicta deleantur nostra delicta."

...

"Credo in Unum Deum, Patrem omnipotentem, factorem cæli et terræ, visibilum omnium, et invisibilium. Et in unum Dominum Jesum Christum, Filium Dei unigenitum. Et ex Patre natum ante omnia sæcla. Deum de Deo, lumen de lumine, Deum verum de Deo vero. Genitum non factum, consubstantialem Patri: per quem omnia facta sunt. Qui propter nos homines, et propter nostram salutem descendit de cælis.

ET INCARNATUS EST DE SPIRITU SANCTO EX MARIA VIRGINE: ET HOMO FACTUS EST. Crucifixus etiam pro nobis: sub Pontio Pilatio passus, et sepultus est. Et resurrexit tertia die, secundum Scripturas. Et ascendit in cælum: sedet ad dextram Patris. Et iterum venetrus est cum gloria judicare vivos et mortuos: cujus regni non erit finis. Et in Spiritum Sanctum, Dominum, et vivificantem: Qui ex Patre, Filioque procedit. Qui cum Patre, et simul adoratur, et conglorificator: qui locutus est per Prophetas. Et unam, sanctam, catholicam et apostolicam Ecclesiam. Confiteor unum baptisma in remissionem peccatorum. Et exspecto resurrectionem mortuorum. Et vitam venturi sæculi. Amen."

. . .

"DEUS, qui humanæ substantiæ dignitatem mirabiliter condidisti . . . da nobis hujus aquæ et vini mysterium, ejus divinitatis esse consortes, qui humanitatis nostræ fieri dignatus est particeps, Jesus Christus Filius tuus, Dominus noster: Qui tecum vivit et regnat in unitate Spiritus Sancti Deus: per omnia sæcula sæculorum. Amen."

. . .

"Lavabo inter innocentes manus meas et cicumdabo altare tuum, Domine . . . Ne perdas cum impiis, Deus, animam meam, et cum viris sanguinum vitam meam . . . Gloria Patri, et Filio, et Spiritui Sancto. Sicut erat in principio, er nunc, et semper: et in sæcula sæculorum. Amen."

"Suscipe, sancta Trinitas, hanc oblationem, quam tib offerimus ob memorium Passoinis, Resurrectionis et Ascensionis Jesu Christi Domini nostri: et in honorem beatæ Mariæ semper Virginis, et beati Joannis Baptistæ, et sanctorum Apostolorum Petri et Pauli, et istorum, et omnum Sanctorum: ut illis proficiat ad honorem nobis intercedere dignentur in cælis, quorum memoriam agimus in terris. Per eumdem Christum Dominum nostrum. Amen."

. . .

"Orate, fratres: ut meum ac vestrum sacrificium acceptabile fiat apud Deum Patrem omnipotentem. *Suscipiat Dominus sacrificium de manibus tuis, ad laudem et gloriam nominis sui, ad utilitatem quoque nostram, totiusque Ecclesiæ suæ sanctæ* Amen."

. . .

"Hoc est enim Corpus meum . . . Simili modo postquam coenatum est, accipiens et hunc præclarum Calicem in sanctas ac venerabiles manus suas: item tibi gratias agens, bene + dixit, deditique discipulis suis, dicens: Accipite, et bibite ex eo omnes. HIC EST ENIM CALIX SANGUINIS MEI, NOVI ET AETRNI TESTAMENTI: MYSTERIUM FIDEI: QUI PRO VOBIS ET PRO MULTUS EFFUNDETUR IN REMISSIONEM PECCATORUM. Hæc quotiescumque feceritis, in mei memoriam facietis."

. . .

"PATER NOSTER, qui es in cælis: Sanctificetur nomen tuum: Adveniat regnum tuum: Fiat voluntas tua, sicut in cælo, et in terra. Panem nostrum quotidianum da nobis hodie: Et dimitte nobis debita nostra, sicut et nos dimittimus debitoribus nostris. Et ne nos inducas in tentatonem. *Sed libera nos a malo.* Amen."

"DOMINE JESU CHRISTE, qui dxisti Apostolis tuis: Pacem relinquo vobis, pacem meam da vobis: ne respicias peccata mea, sed fidem Ecclesiæ tuæ: eamque secumdum voluntatem tuum pacificare et coadunare digneris: Qui vivis et regnas Deus per per omnia sæcula sæculorum. Amen. "

...Corpus Domini nostri Jesu Christi custodiat animam meam in vitam æternam. Amen."

...Ecce Agnus Dei: ecce qui tollit peccata mundi. *Domine, non sum dignus, ut intres sub tectum meum : sed tantum dic verbo, et sanabitur anima mea.* Corpus Domini Jesu Christi custodiat animam tuam in vitam æternam. Amen..."

. . .

"Dominus vobiscum."

"Et cum spiritu tuo."

I flip through some well-worn pages to find my place in the Missal. I don't have the responses memorized yet.

"Ite, Missa est," Father LeBron says.

"Deo gratias."

"Placeat tibi, sancta Trinitas, obsequium servitutis meæ: et præsta; ut sacrificium, quod oculis tuæ majestatis indignus obtuli, tibi sit acceptabile, mihique, et omnibus pro quibis illud obtuli, sit, te miserante, propitiabile. Per Christum Dominum nostrum. Amen."

Father LeBron then raises his right hand, soon setting it in motion to make the sweeping sign through the still air. "Benedictat vos omnipotens Deus, Pater, et Filius, et Spiritus Sanctus."

"Amen."

Mass, concluded—*Hail, Holy Queen, 3 Hail Mary's,* the *Saint Michael the Archangel* prayer prayed—Father LeBron hands them the lessonspacket for quick review and says,

'Look, here's some golden ones on time and eternity and, guys, as we're wrapping up and, rather even still, *have already,* wrapped up, let's just pop that top and drink deep for a final time from those two lodestar books of his. You already know: that *City of God* and, yep, that other one: *Confessions.* The way Augustine drops us right into the deep well filled to the brim with the bluest and coldest and most eminently potable waters concerning that for God (I AM who AM,[94] all time is NOW), God does not have a present or future but only an ETERNAL PRESENT and therefore is master of time, of space, of everything—"...yet if the present were always present, it would not pass into the past: it would not be time but eternity..."[95]—is epic, legit, based beyond belief and simply, most importantly, true. This mastery is witnesses-able by us and all of creation: "We adore God who made heaven and earth and all that they contain, God who made every kind of soul, from the lowest that lives without sensation and intellection through the sentient up to the soul that can think."[96] Indeed, concerning God: "...ours [years] come and go so that all may come in succession. All your years subsist in simultaneity, because they do not change...your years are one day.'[97]

'So, yes, goldmine: all of his writing.
A few more on time:'

---

[94] Exodus 3:14; St. Augustine, *The City of God* (New York: Image/ Doubleday, 1958), XII, chpt 2, 246.

[95] St. Augustine, *Confessions* (OUP, trans. Henry Chadwick, 1991), XI, 231.

[96] St. Augustine, *The City of God* (New York: Image/Doubleday, 1958), VII, chpt 29, 139

[97] St. Augustine, *Confessions* (OUP, trans. Henry Chadwick, 1991), XI, 231.

This is my reply to anyone who asks: "What was God doing before He made Heaven and Earth?" My reply is not that which someone is said to have given as a joke to evade the force of the question. He said, "He was preparing hells for people who inquire into profundities."[98]

It is one thing to laugh, and another to see the point at issue, and this reply I reject. I would have preferred him to answer, "I am ignorant of what I do not know" rather than reply so as to ridicule someone who has asked a deep question and to win approval for an answer which is a mistake. No, I say that you, our God, are the Creator of every created being, and assuming that by "heaven and earth" is meant every created thing I boldly declare: Before God made heaven and earth, he was not making anything. If he was making anything, it could only be something created.[99]

However, God also foresaw that a community of saints would be called to supernatural adoption, would have their sins forgiven, be sanctified by the Holy Spirit, and finally be united with the holy angels in eternal peace so that, at last, the enemy death will be destroyed. And God knew how good it would be for this community often to recall that the human race had its roots in one man, precisely to show how pleasing it is to God that men, though many, should be one.[100]

There was therefore no time when you had not made something, because you made time itself. No times are coeternal with you since you are permanent. If they were permanent they would not be times.[101]

---

[98] Like a joke the Venerable Abp. Fulton Sheen once told a crowd. Basically—and to make a long story short and paraphrasing too—some guy didn't believe Jonah actually got swallowed by a whale and kept badgering Bishop Sheen about it and finally Sheen said, 'Look, sure, I can't tell you exactly how it happened. When I get to Heaven, I'll ask him.' The guy responded with, *what if Jonah is not in Heaven and so you cannot ask him?* Sheen shot back, 'then you ask him.'

[99] St. Augustine, *Confessions* (OUP, trans. Henry Chadwick, 1991), XI, 229.

[100] St. Augustine, *The City of God* (New York: Image/Doubleday, 1958), XII, chpt 23, 263.

[101] St. Augustine, *Confessions* (OUP, trans. Henry Chadwick, 1991), XI, 230.

Father LeBron then said they should remember this about Augustine on time. Eternity is not, as many imagine it, endless time or so much time, 29 trillion years, for example. Rather, it is the total absence of time. It is 11:15AM on a Thursday morning frozen like a photograph forever, unchanging. Its non-time character is precisely what makes it eternal.

Then they reviewed all the lessons.
Silently, to
themselves.
For Father LeBron had handed them each a packet,
blue in color, the cover, the inside pages white. Blue
ink for the headings, the rest in black. And he said, 'take,
and read.' There were 100 points they should take from
their spiritual advising. Here they were, in one packet.
Take and read.
And so, they did.

. . . .

For Mark and Anna, my friends.
In Christ, yours,

—Father LeBron

The FULL RECAP of our SIX LESSONS

_____ points in running tally

100, in sum.

____

1. the City of God v. the City of Man

There are three features of the City of Man, the bad stuff, and I want you to avoid them. Bad stuff that 1. corrodes the soul, 2. breaks you down and reduces you, even if at first slowly, into a shell of yourself multiplied by many shells until 3. one day you wake up and you're right there, standing on the precipice of hell itself.

Yes, learn these and then avoid them:

4. Gossip and calumny and a refusal to mind one's own business.
5. Cringy political caricatures
6. Putting hope in earthly princes, which is the ultimate building your house on sand not stone thing...do you understand?
7. [102] avoid City of Man things, seek the City of God, and be assured that seeking first the Kingdom of God, and His righteousness, God will give you all good things besides.

8. the Problem of Evil

9. Evil does not have a positive nature.
10. Evil is lack, privation, deprivation, the absence of a good that should be there but is not.
11. Evil therefore is not something, in and of itself, but something missing.

---

[102] #4 here #7 total/overall —Fr. LB.

12. Evil, defect, can only be talked about in reference to the good. God, all good, made all things good. There is only a first, foundational source of good: God, and all God made, again, is good. This Great Good made all goods, plural. There is no original great Bad making small bads. For, back to 9 through 11, evil does not have a positive nature or source, it is only the corruption, the rot, the lack of the original good. Reinforcing this,

13. Good can exist without evil but not the other way around. Without sin, which is the source of evil, our own corrupted wills willing defect, all things would be wholly good, as they should have been, as is their natural state. All things good, all things integrally operating as they were meant to. But evil can only come into existence off of the good, in response to the good, in corruption of the good. The worst evil, the most bad bad, Hell, is this to the maximum: full evil because a complete corruption of good, a complete lacking of the good and so what results is utter and perpetual darkness.

14. is the definition of evil straight from the horse's mouth. How does St. Augustine himself define evil in his magisterial *City of God?* I've read this book cover to cover 58 times, and had it memorized after the 27th read, so I will provide the definition and page citation. P.s.,' Father Lebron says, pulling out the book and throwing it Mark, who catches it against his chest, 'it's yours. My personal annotated copy. As you can see: the slightly abridged, introduction by Etienne Gilson, 1958 Image/ Doubleday Edition, 551 pages into the Index, absolutely ridiculously pretty seafoam green cover with that nice, very yellow sun too. That's what I'll be citing from.'

15. —p. 217, Book XI, chapter nine, Saint Augustine, quote: 'Evil has no positive nature; what we call evil is merely the lack of something that is good.'

And one more definition, for good measure, here from
16. Book XIV, chapter 11, p. 305, St Augustine quote, 'evil
cannot exist without good, since the natures to which the
defects belong, in as much as they are natures, are good.'

General lacks

17. In ability to learn music/as in or, learn stuff period.
18. Physical, as in sports or sporting, fails.
19. Small cough, common cold, breakdown of the body.
20. Lacks in etiquette and interpersonal behavior.
21. On beauty.

The more serious stuff

22. Lack of familial love
23. Lack of charity towards the poor
24. Physical ailments (here a bigger breakdown than
above in D.3)
25. Crimes, large and small
26. Wars
27. 'Ok, so, guys, my friends, look, this then brings us to
Why is their evil? Why does God allow evil? What
is the point, anyways?

First, I think we have to understand, and rejoice,
in the fact that we are not God and whereas He is
not bound by time and space but the possessor of
an Eternal, unchanging vision, we are, and so we
don't know how it all fits together and maybe even
some things we think are bad are not in fact bad
but we just don't see how it all fits together and all
we can do, as men and women of faith, is trust God.
Live that Divine Mercy image motto, 'Jesus, I trust
in You' and that fruit of the first sorrowful mystery,
the Agony in the Garden, resignation to God's will.

God has a plan, for you personally, and *the* plan,
in general, too. The victory has already been won,

but we have to do our part and say yes to Him and trust in Him. And remember,

28.

Romans 8:28—and we know that all things work together for good for those who love God, who are called according to his purpose.

But if you want even a little more than that, in conclusion,' Father LeBron says, 'I'd say that God (29.) ultimately allows evil only to bring about a greater good. In the book of Genesis, Joseph, he never becomes Egyptian Grain Czar and Prime Minister without first being thrown in a cistern by his moron brothers. Their evil brought about a greater good and Joseph even says this, it's right there in Genesis, that the evil they wished to do to him has been turned by God into good. God ultimately allows evil only to bring about a greater good. And it's tied up in our free will. We have free will, listen to what St Augustine says about that: "God is the Cause of all causes, although not of all choices (Book V, chapter 8, p. 103)" and "Man's will is all important. If it is badly directed, the emotions will be perverse; if it is rightly directed, the emotions will be not merely blameless but praiseworthy.' (Book XIV, chapter 6, p.303).

And so, because we have (30.) free will, we can say no and we did, Adam and Eve did. That's the origin of evil, the original deprivation, choosing not God, choosing a defective destiny apart from God. But from that evil, what comes? A greater good. (31.) The Incarnation, the Word Made flesh and dwelling among us, the God-Man, perfectly innocent, suffering the apparent greatest evil in human history, Deicide, God crucified by his sinful and rebellious creation, but all this only to bring about the greatest good: Easter Sunday, Eternal Glory, for, amen,

amen again: dying you destroyed our death, Rising you restored our life. Saint Augustine said, Felix Culpa, and he was right.

He was absolutely right.'

32. Attractions and Attachments

33. Resentment is like drinking poison and waiting for the other person to die.
34. This is the very perfection of a man, to find out his own imperfections.
35. Beauty is indeed a good gift of God; but that the good may not think it a great good, God dispenses it even to the wicked.
36. The desire for fame tempts even noble minds.
37. As to those feebler spirits who, though they cannot be said to prefer earthly possessions to Christ, do yet cleave to them with a somewhat immoderate attachment, they have discovered by the pain of losing these things how much they were sinning in loving them. For their grief is of their own making.
38. God is always trying to give good things to us, but our hands are too full to receive them.
39. Thus, a good man, though a slave, is free; but a wicked man, though a king, is a slave. For he serves, not one man alone, but what is worse, as many masters as he has vices.

40. Chastity

41.

My lesson ~~will come~~ came in three parts: (41.–43)

A. What Saint Augustine said.

B. Chronicling the Cringe, with a (parenthetical note 'so as to reject it')

C. Positive prescriptions

44.

"The more unscrupulous I was, the greater my reputation was likely to be, for men are so blind that they even take pride in their blindness."

45.

"What an abomination! What a parody of life! What abysmal death! Could I enjoy doing wrong for no other reason than that it was wrong?"

46.

"Even though it clings to things of beauty, if their beauty is outside God and outside the soul, it only clings to sorrow."

47.

"The truth, of course, was that it was all my own self, and my own impiety had divided me against myself. My sin was all the more incurable because I did not think myself a sinner.

48.

"I lived in misery, like every man whose soul is tethered by the love of things that cannot last and then is agonized to lose them."

49.

"But my sin was this, that I looked for pleasure, beauty, and truth not in him but in myself and his other creatures, and the search led me instead to pain, confusion, and error."

50.

"Grant me chastity, Lord, just not yet."

51.

All my empty dreams suddenly lost their charm and my heart began to throb with a bewildering passion for the wisdom of eternal truth."

52.

"To fall in love with God is the greatest romance; to seek Him is the greatest adventure; to find Him, the greatest human achievement."

53. Chastity is super important. Wait till you're married. Be faithful to your spouse. Be open to life.
54. Chastity is super important. Wait till you're married. Be faithful to your spouse. Be open to life.
55. Chastity is super important. Wait till you're married. Be faithful to your spouse. Be open to life.
56. be aloof, a good aloof:
>You gotta give one word answers.
>Yes.
>No.
>I don't know.
>Nah.
>Yep.
>None of your business.
57. Read *Theology of the Body* and/or *... for dummies.*
58. pre-Cana classes marriage prep
59. be normal.

60. Donatism and Proto-Protestantism

61. Hence the sacraments give her visible character to the Church, and. in a sense, build her up externally.
62. the Church as the Body of Christ, as an invisible and spiritual organization. The sacrament which most especially makes possible this spiritual unity in Christ's Body is. of course, the Eucharist.
63. The Eucharist is our daily bread, and our power for good which is shown forth therein, is unity. That is to say that we are made into his own body; and having been made into his body, we ourselves become what we receive.
64. The Church as a whole received the gift of the Holy Spirit. The sinner has offended the whole people of God and must be reconciled to them if he wishes to live again in the Holy Spirit of God.
65. Lazarus is compared with a sinner. Both are dead until the grace of Christ calls out to them. Yet even after

"coming forth," both are "bound." As the disciples loosed Lazarus from his bandages, they must loose the sinner from his guilt. Augustine had shown that the entire Church possessed radically the power of binding and loosing sinners: Has *enim claves non homo unus, sed unitas accepit Ecclesiae.* Here he indicates that the grace of God initiates the process of repentance and forgiveness.

66. It should be mentioned in passing that Augustine places considerable emphasis in the Lazarus parallel on the private confession of sins to the bishop. Through this action the sinner "comes forth" from the tomb even though he is still bound. It is the first step in the sinner's return to peace with the Church and thereby with God.

67. Satisfaction for sin must be made to the Church as well as to God. Consequently, the bishops are empowered to assign periods of penance depending upon the gravity of the sin.

68. What you see is the bread and the chalice; that is what your own eyes report to you. But what your faith obliges you to accept is that the bread is the body of Christ and the chalice is the blood of Christ. This has been said very briefly, which may perhaps be sufficient for faith; yet faith does not desire instruction.

69. We do not sin when we adore Christ in the Eucharist; we do sin when we do not adore Christ in the Eucharist.

70. Christ held Himself in His hands when He gave His Body to His disciples saying: 'This is My Body.' No one partakes of this Flesh before he has adored it.

71. I had promised those of you who have just been baptized a sermon to explain the sacrament of the Lord's table, which you can see right now, and which you shared in last night. You ought to know what you have received, what you are about to receive, what you ought to receive every day. That bread which you can see on the altar, sanctified by the word of God, is the body of Christ. That cup, or rather what the cup contains, sanctified by the word of God, is the blood of Christ.

72. "Not the visible sun, but the invisible Creator of the sun has consecrated this day on which the Virgin, a true but inviolate Mother, gave birth to Him who became visible for our sake and by whom she herself was created. A virgin conceives, yet remains a virgin: a virgin is heavy with child; a virgin brings forth her child, yet she is always a virgin. Why are you amazed at this, O man? It was fitting for God to be born thus when He deigned to become man."

73. Already in the writings of the Bishop of Hippo, the idea of the predestination of Mary appeared. Recently, the Magisterium, in the Bull Munificentissimus Deus from Pius XII, stated that Mary was chosen in the same moment that God decided for the Word to become Incarnate. In the 5th century, Augustine said, "He knew His mother in predestination, even before He was born of her; even before, as God, He created her of whom, as man, He was to be created, He knew her as His mother' (Trac. In Iohanem 8,9). 'He chose the Mother he had created; he created the Mother he had chosen.'

74. Having excepted the Holy Virgin Mary, concerning whom, on account of the honor of the Lord, I wish to have absolutely no question when treating of sins—for how do we know what abundance of grace for the total overcoming of sin was conferred upon her, who merited to conceive and bear him in whom there was no sin?—so, I say, with the exception of the Virgin, if we could have gathered together all those holy men and women, when they were living here, and had asked them whether they were without sin, what do we suppose would have been their answer?'

75. "Next, the Lord's Prayer is said which you have already received and recited. Why is it said before receiving the Body and Blood of Christ? Because of our human frailty perhaps our minds imagined something which is not becoming, our eyes saw something which was not decent, our ears heard something exaggeratedly which

was not fitting. If perhaps such things have been kept in because of temptation and the fragility of human life, they are washed away by the Lord's Prayer at the moment we say, 'Forgive us our trespasses' so that we can safely approach the sacrament."

76. No one can have God as his Father who does not have the Church as his mother.

77. I would not believe in the Gospel if the authority of the Catholic Church did not bid me to do so.

78. The custom of Mother Church in baptizing infants is certainly not to be scorned, nor is it to be regarded in any way as superfluous, nor is it to be believed that its tradition is anything except apostolic.

79. Wicked sons do not have the Holy Ghost in the same way as do beloved sons, and yet they do have Baptism. So, too, heretics do not have the Church as Catholics have, even though they have Baptism.

80. There is nothing more serious than the sacrilege of schism because there is no just cause for severing the unity of the Church.

81.
SAINT AUGUSTINE WAS NOT A PROTESTANT.
HE'S ONE OF OURS.
KICK ROCKS, PUNCH WALLS.

HE'S CATHOLIC.

82.
SAINT AUGUSTINE WAS NOT A PROTESTANT.
HE'S ONE OF OURS.
KICK ROCKS, PUNCH WALLS.

HE'S CATHOLIC.
83.
SAINT AUGUSTINE WAS NOT A PROTESTANT.
HE'S ONE OF OURS.
KICK ROCKS, PUNCH WALLS.

HE'S CATHOLIC.

84.
SAINT AUGUSTINE WAS NOT A PROTESTANT.
HE'S ONE OF OURS.
KICK ROCKS, PUNCH WALLS.

HE'S CATHOLIC.

85.
SAINT AUGUSTINE WAS NOT A PROTESTANT.
HE'S ONE OF OURS.
KICK ROCKS, PUNCH WALLS.

HE'S CATHOLIC.

86.
SAINT AUGUSTINE WAS NOT A PROTESTANT.
HE'S ONE OF OURS.
KICK ROCKS, PUNCH WALLS.

HE'S CATHOLIC.

87.
SAINT AUGUSTINE WAS NOT A PROTESTANT.
HE'S ONE OF OURS.
KICK ROCKS, PUNCH WALLS.

HE'S CATHOLIC.

88. Your choice, Mark and Anna. And the president said they said this to him because according to him, the president, they, the aliens, are huge fans of Saint Augustine of Hippo. They're all about free will. You have to deal with the consequences of the free choices you make, but you are free.

89. On Time and the Eternal Now

***—the one time we did not DO THE LESSONS, we
90. LIVED THEM.
　　Guys,
　　Read all you want about Saint Augustine and time.
　　There's a lot.

91. Read, *City of God;* you already have.

See: some say he, Augustine, invented the 'concept of time.' Teleology, goals, the ultimate goal, time not some stupid spinning, probably broken, wheel. No. God outside of time and space therefore 92. Master of it.

93. Eternity: not endless time but the absence of time.

94. Time: use it or lose it. And you, we, us, we have, may

95. God help us and 96. have mercy upon us, used it.

97. Time = the 2 pluses. You got all these recap points from our spiritual advising lessons, then here's the two pluses.

Time-= 2 pluses

+1, pray

+2, work.

You (98.) prayed, you (99.) worked, that, when built

Upon

(100.) God's grace,

the

Only foundation, is the recipe for

Perfection.

. . . .

. . . .

. . . . Be assured of my

prayers. And please pray for me,

FR. LB.

. . . .

The trip from the Old-Moscow Pullman Highway to the moon was far more normal than either Mark or Anna had expected. A classic, so much out of central casting it was almost boring, or annoying, saucer shape UFO had descended on the glassy, frozen pond of the former dirt road and green men—no, seriously, though: that's what they look like: about 5'4, muscular beyond belief, imagine a 5'4, 330 pound man with less than 5% body fat and looking like he can flat foot 60 inch vertical, like he can broad jump kangaroo style 25 feet and dunk threes, like he runs a sub 3.8 40. These guys, from first impression, look far more impressive than Oneofthemones and SoCooked, Mark's imagined, virtual reality players. They're fake, Mark's guys, these green guys, they're real—and so yeah, four green men exited the UFO and walked up to Mark and Anna and after about two or three seconds of silence one of them said,

'Let's go.'

Mark and Anna made a start for the ship but another one drew it out longer.

'Let's goooooooo,' extending his arms and hands, all green, all of them this bright green like the old plastic army guys used to be. Bright green like the old Philadelphia Eagles uniforms of the mid 1970s; not hunter green, not any kind of dark green, no.

Bright, light, almost shiny green.

Mark and Anna just stood there.

'Excuse me,' one of the aliens said. 'I mean, forgive me, I beg, *we* beg your pardon. "Let's go"' is my people's way of greeting, bidding farewell, expressing satisfaction and affection. It is a very flexible word. I believe it is similar to the way Americans employ "love." I love my dog, I love my wife, I love Havarti cheese, I love poems and walks by the seashore.'

'Why "let's go"?' Mark asked.

'Because of the TV show *Gen Z House*,' the alien replied.

'*Gen Z House?*' Anna asked, looking at Mark. He's never heard of it either.

The four aliens groaned loudly.

'What?,' another one asked. 'No, you cannot be serious. You do not know this television program, available on our planet in all four reception methods, CCN, tele-YT, BC 5, and inverted foamstream?'

Mark and Anna shook their heads.

'*Gen Z House.*'

'Sorry,' Mark said.

'Look, allow me to explain as briefly as I can, for we must be on our way, and with all deliberate haste. Our culture is technologically superior to yours. But American *culture*, or what the Germans used to call *kultur*, in what you refer to as the "fin de siècle" period immediately preceding the First World War on your planet, now, of that, American culture, we are, as you say, "big fans." *Gen Z House* was a . . . ' the alien paused, searching for the right words, looking to his friends.

'Reality show,' another alien said.

'Right, yes. A reality show that followed the everyday exploits of late teenage, early twenty something college students in the United States of America many years ago. I do not remember how long ago, please, I must once again beg your pardon, for we mark the passing of time on our planet much differently than you do. These students were college young men and women on a region called the Palouse—aha, see, right here, so you see why we have come here and flooded unto ice all this here—college students on the Palouse attending the University of Idaho and Washington State University and, despite their asynchronous matriculations, they lived together in a, a, fraternity and sorority combined into one. *Gen Z House.* I, myself, loved the enthusiasm of all the students, the love they had for their schools. "Go Vandals!" "Go Cats!" '

'Cougs,' the other alien who before knew what a reality show was said.

'Cougs?' the narrating one asked, looking confused. 'Are you certain?'

'Yes.'

'Really? I distinctly remember the rallying cry of the school in Pullman being Cats, "Go Cats!" '

'No.'

'Are you sure?'

Mark is now visibly annoyed. 'He's right, it's "Go Cougs!" '

'Oh...okay. Well, shall we?' motioning for them to board the flying saucer.

Mark looked at Anna. She nodded. She seemed cool with it. Or, maybe, it's just, *let's get this over with.*

The flight to the moon was memorable for its speed above all. Roughly twenty-seven minutes from take-off to touch down.

And so **presently**, look out your window and look down, **now**:

They land onto an airstrip that seems laid out in the very middle of a large, football-like, perhaps even NASCAR-like, stadium. The Circus Maximus in Space.

'How many people,' Marks says, 'I mean—

'No,' the main alien says, 'it's the same, yes, we say people too.'

'You call yourselves "people"?'

'Yes. Well, actually, it's actually something, well, quite long in our language but "people," "people" is the literal translation.'

'Try me,' Mark says.

'Try you? Try what?'

'Tell me the real name. I want to see if I can pronounce it.'

'Okay,' the alien says. 'It's "ghfjkfhjkhkfhekwhdjwehykj wefuebfu3ybjje8723ub23u203eboy823yr38r787837r873r873r8 2befjbejbjhjkhdkjqwhdkjwh83y8ry23iru23uhr238r2387837r jbfjefjhwdkjhwefliwjufio3oufhefjhwjehkjhwkdjhwokury23 iuh2u3hr273r982uy3ohf2oif2ofh2flkehdlkjldkjqwlkdjlkgiu 2efgkjwghefkgwieufgi2ugtyryu3uyr2uy3r8273r892389ry2iu fg2i786232hekdjhqwldjkhqljkwhdlqwhdlqhwlfheklfhlwkh dlqwdhlqkwjfwueghi2367r67368r723908u230899012e1o9ih wdlkwoifhwekjfbqwjbndkjbwkjhwdkjgwkh." But, just like how in your language there is a silent h or a silent k, in "ghfjkfhjkhkfhekwhdjwehykjwefuebfu3ybjje8723ub23u2 03eboy823yr38r787837r873r873r82befjbejbjhjkhdkjqwhdkjw h83y8ry23iru23uhr238r2387837rjbfjefjhwdkjhwefliwjufio3o ufhefjhwjehkjhwkdjhwokury23iuh2u3hr273r982uy3ohf2oi f2ofh2flkehdlkjldkjqwlkdjlkgiu2efgkjwghefkgwieufgi2ugt yryu3uyr2uy3r8273r892389ry2iufg2i786232hekdjhqwldjkhq ljkwhdlqwhdlqhwlfheklfhlwkhdlqwdhlqkwjfwueghi2367r 67368r723908u230899012e1o9ihwdlkwoifhwekjfbqwjbndk jbwkjhwdkjgwkh" the "2i786232hekdjhqwldjkhqljkwhdlqwhdlqhw" is silent.'

'Wow,' Mark says. 'Okay, got it. So, how many people are here?'

'800,000.'

'800,000,' Anna says. 'For us? For this?'

The alien nods. 'If you thought you were popular on Earth, and you are, double it, maybe triple it, amongst my people. Words cannot express our gratitude for your agreeing to come and do a show. 800,000 in person and more than 12.5 billion watching live on various co-temporalportation streaming dissimulators.'

What happened next was so usual, so second nature, so typical, even quotidian, it was near shocking in the juxtaposed dislocation from the standard (modeling) to the non-standard (the on the moon setting, in a show hosted by aliens).

Mark and Anna walked runaways alone, together, and atop various animals. The aliens had temporarily manipulated the moon's atmosphere to make it Earth inhabitable; fine-tuned to Des Moines, Iowa in late May, the main alien told Mark sometime during the show. They modeled atop lions and tigers and bears, oh my[103], astride matching elephants, in between alligators, and on a sled pulled by a pack of Rottweilers with little baby Rottweilers, puppies, on top of the sled-pulling big Rottweilers. Suffice to say, it was a lot of Rottweilers. If you like Rottweilers, you'd love this. If you've ever woken up and thought, 'I'd really love to see some Rottweilers today,' this day would be a day chalk full of memories. You'd probably circle that day in your daily planner and even cross out the date, let's say February 20th, and write in its place, in bold font, ROTT-WEILER DAY. It was a lot of Rottweilers, that's for sure.

After each and every set the stadium exploded with thunderous choruses of 'let's gooooooooooooo!'

The crowd demanded an encore and then another. A planned three-hour showed extended to four hours

---

[103] Please see: *The Wizard of Oz*, dir. Victor Fleming, starring Judy Garland, et al (Metro-Goldwyn-Mayer, 1939).

and 27 minutes. The main alien told Anna and Mark that they could be transported back down to Earth in ten minutes—it was longer from Earth to the moon, he explained, then from the moon back down and it had to do with the technology of their ships, 'in particular the . . . never mind . . .

. . . do you guys want to leave now, or get some rest and then leave first thing in the morning?'

For Mark and Anna, there was no question as to what they should do. A ticker tape parade of embarrassing proportions awaited them back on Earth. They had saved the planet, after all. So probably billions of people welcoming them back, watching them arrive on the Moscow Pullman Highway as the extraterrestrial people had watched them arrive here. Presidential speeches and medals, accolades aplenty, interviews and the ever-obnoxious question: 'so does this mean the two of you are back to modeling, full time? Can we drop the "former" from your professional titles?'

No, you see, all that could wait. Especially when the main alien explained that Mark and Anna were to be put up in something called the anti-Gravity suite, which included a moonrock lined hot tub, the water heated from 'Jupiter stones,' whatever that was, and the very best 'alien wine,' which sold, on this guy's planet, for the Earth equivalent of 17,000$ a bottle. *No, but, okay, but, wait,* Mark said, *wait, what is it actually called, the 'alien wine,' not this translated simplification.* 'Alien wine,' the alien explained, further noting, 'this name makes it very marketable in other galaxies. We think it will do very well on Earth once alien and Earth people relations, even diplomatic relations I might say, are normalized,' which he, the alien, conceded, might be quite challenging considering the facts. The facts being these aliens showed up to Earth and skipping over any and all pleasantries and formalities threatened to blow up the Earth. But, you know, he said, slapping Mark on the shoulder, you guys, meaning Mark and Anna, you guys 'fixed it, you know, so . . . we're good now, right?'

Mark and Anna said nothing.

The alien said he would ask his leader, the alien king or something, and the president of the United States, to make Mark First Ambassador to the Extraterrestrial Territories, something like that and what did he, Mark, think of that? Mark didn't say anything. Anna looked very proud of Mark, proud in the classic, *my man, that's my man!*, type way.

Mark and Anna enjoyed their night in the anti-Gravity suite, maybe even a little too much. Well-oiled on alien wine they took turns singing, a capella, as many national anthems as they could manage, working their way down in alphabetical order. They were singing so loudly that they were keeping nearby aliens up and these guys, despite being huge fans for sure, where starting to think, 'so when are they going to shut up already?'

Having made it to Iceland they could proceed no further.

Anna burst out into tears.

'What is it?' Mark asked her. 'Are you okay?'

'No,' she said, 'no,' sobbing, head in her hands. 'Why do you love me? Why? I mean you . . . you could have picked anyone but you . . . but . . . but you settled for me. And what if I stop being beautiful, what if I like, like let myself go, like,' sobbing again.

Mark started laughing. But before he could tell her the very plain and obvious truth: that it was he that was the lucky one, wow, praise God, that he, model though he was, struggled with his own self-esteem issues as all men, as all people do, and no, look, girl, no, you've got it all wrong, I am the lucky one. I'm married to Anna

Davenport. I landed Anna Davenport and made her, wow, made her Anna Dupont. You just don't get it, you don't understand how I, it is me, I, I'm the lucky one, before he could say all that she was already asleep, passed out, out cold, lying on the floor like she'd been tucked in snug hours ago, tongue just drooping out of her mouth as she snored loudly and steadily.

Mark picked her up off the floor and unfurled the sheets and tucked her in and covered her up like she liked and kissed her on the head and resumed laughing. He really was so lucky. So blessed.

He stood up and walked out into the lunar air on the grand balcony of the anti-Gravity suite. He could see Mars suspended in the **far-off blackness** like a red skittle dropped on a wool sweater. He took all this in. He was on the moon, now confirmed as one of the two greatest models in all of history, having completed the greatest fashion show in the history of the Milky Way Galaxy, and to rave reviews. To incredible hype, and under considerable geopolitical slash existential and extraterrestrial pressure beforehand; but he, they, had delivered. And the most beautiful woman in the world was asleep but a few feet away and she was his, his wife. And he'd be returning to Earth the way Caesar had returned from Gaul; expect grander, in much grander fashion . . .

. . . he paused. . . .

taking all this in. . . .

he thought of Father LeBron, and he thought of Saint Augustine of Hippo and all those invaluable lessons he and Anna had learned, and he thought of the book the two of them were now going to write, and he thought of all this influence, and the influence brought to bear on their book, and the way in which it would make people fall in love with Saint Augustine, that then making them fall in love with Christ and His Church, that then being, that then was, no, look, is, it is and would be as in will be, just very, very cool...

To God be the glory, all the glory, amen.

Mark then pulled out a rosary from his pocket and thought: *I'm going to be the first person in human history to pray a Rosary on the Moon.* And that too, that was cool.

He blessed himself, looked out at the stars once more, and
started praying.

About the Author

Gracjan Kraszewski is the author of the novels *Thermonuclear Mirth, Seraphim and the Dust Plague,* and *The Holdout;* the book of essays, *The Hippo Lectures;* the Civil War history, *Catholic Confederates.* Director of Intellectual Formation at the Saint Augustine Center (Vandal Catholic) in Moscow, Idaho, he holds a PhD in history from Mississippi State University, and has taught, and currently teaches, at universities in the Midwest (formerly) and Pacific Northwest (presently).

Kraszewski played baseball in college, professionally in Europe in the Czech and Belgian premier leagues, and for the Polish National Team. Like Father LeBron, he enjoys deadlifting and dunking, maxing at 605 lbs in the deadlift and dunking on a rim as high at 10′5″. Fluent in English, Polish, and French, he also speaks, to some degree of competency, Italian, Russian, and Spanish. He's online at the YouTube channel 'MapleGracjan-Syrup.' Playlists include the longform historical themed 'Maple Syrup History,' catechetical themed 'Catholic Topics Talks,' and where *Mark and Anna,* as it was performed live, can be found: 'Hippo Lectures.'

Mark and Anna, Models is Kraszewski's fourth novel and sixth book overall. He is currently researching for a comprehensive history of people on the Palouse during the Great War. Two other works of fiction are completed—a poetry/prose story called *Bubbba's Purgatorio* inspired by Dante's *Divine Comedy* and the story of journalist in 2060s America called *Margaux Himmel*—but currently in a first draft stage. He envisions, and hopes, these three might see publication sometime between 2026-2028. His immediate, next Hippo Lecture inspired 6-chapter fiction, which he hopes to give live in 2025-2026, and has just begun writing, takes place in a WINCO supermarket and is called, *The Grocery Store Past the Garden of Eden.*

The Andrew and Elizabeth Introduction(s) Appendix

1. The City of God v. the City of Man [1]

Elizabeth: Good evening, my name is Elizabeth.

Andrew: And I'm Andrew. I sometimes also go by Pete.

Elizabeth: You can call me Betty.

Andrew: I also go by Wilson, Davis, and Toblerone.

Elizabeth: My family calls my Bunty. Well, except for my great-grama. She calls me Mom.

Andrew: Think of me as the 1950s TV dinner Dad. Hey, Dolores, the lite beer's not gonna refill itself! And what time is *Twilight Zone* on again?

Elizabeth: I love watching Twilight Zone but only when it's actually twilight. 10 minutes to sundown? Count me in. Other times? No, no thank you.

Andrew: As Delphine was saying, speaking of watching things . . .

Elizabeth: Right. Thanks, Jeremy. Tonight we have for you the first Hippo Lecture of the semester. A story of a man, a woman, a first date, and an unexpected guest

---

[1] (that which was read by the aforementioned Andrew and Elizabeth immediately prior to the talk. The order being Me: free intro, A&E: official, gold standard intro, Me: Return and dive right in. . . . please rinse and repeat this same formula—aka Ibid-through the A&E appendix for Nos. 2–6).

showing up with a well worn copy of St. Augustine's *City of God* and . . . off we go.

Andrew: Horses out gate, pedal to the metal, Vin Diesel, Paul Walker, models modeling, greyhound dogs at the track running, fast, spoiler alert: they're trying to win. And this story, should you follow its trajectory to the finish line will show you how to work towards the winning side City of God behaviors while avoiding disqualifying City of Man mishaps along the way.

2. The Problem of Evil

(Elizabeth alone for this one)

Ladies and Gentlemen:

Welcome to our second Hippo lecture of the year and the second chapter of a book, to be completed in spring, 2025, called *The Adventures of Mark and Anna; Models,* explorations of St Augustine's writings through a postmodern setting and style.

Last month we heard about the City of God v. the City of Man. Tonight's theme is: the Problem of Evil. What is evil, why does it exist, what is its character, what can be done? Mark and Anna will once more, and throughout this series, have this explained to them by their spiritual advisor, the good Father Lebron. But the explanations only coming after we pick up with Mark and Anna's story following their wedding, they now on honeymoon at Heyburn State Park. Mark and Anna: what could have been had Aeneas and Dido worked out.

3. Attractions and Attachments

Elizabeth: Tonight's talk is part 3 of the book, *Mark and Anna: Former (?) Models: Reflections on the timeless Wisdom of Saint Augustine of Hippo through a postmodern prism.*

Andrew: Having heard their spiritual advisor Father Lebron's instructions concerning the 'City of God vs. the City of Man,' and 'The Problem of Evil,' Mark and Anna return, once more, to the Old Moscow Pulman Highway for session 3.

Elizabeth: 'Attractions and Attachments,' is the topic of this session 3. The pesky, everyday life stuff—like cellphones, movies, social media—up to the more serious and disordered attachments that, whether great or small keep us from God.

Andrew: Hey, Elizabeth check this out (pull out cellphone and show her something)

Elizabeth: No way!

—**Actor's note:** *Proceed to literally spend 20-30 seconds engrossed in phone, laughing, whatever, as if you were the only people in the world, while up on stage and make no comment as you just, after these 30 seconds, return to your seats. --*

4. Chastity

Elizabeth walks up to Andrew, who is seated, working a PlayStation controller in his hands, looking out at the audience as if there was a TV screen/video game console.

Elizabeth: Hey, so do you wanna go to the Catholic chastity conference?

Andrew: No.

Elizabeth: C'mon, it's in Spokane. How often do we get something like this so close?

Andrew: Don't care. No.

Elizabeth: Why?

Andrew: It's gonna be lame.

Elizabeth: Lame?

(Andrew all the time, while speaking, playing the video game)

Andrew: Super Lame. Extremely Cringe. Cliché ridden. Obvious things like $1 + 1 = 2$ but said with over the top and unnecessary enthusiasm. I'll pass, thanks.

Elizabeth: Well, what do we do then? How do we, you know, stay fortified in the wedding vows we made ... do we just read *Theology of the Body* on repeat forever?

(Andrew hands Elizabeth the controller. She sits down and starts 'playing the game')

Andrew: No. Here's what we do. We go and see that priest everyone is saying can explain old things in new ways; can make you hear something you've heard a hundred times like it's the first time. Father Lebron. I bet he'll have something to say about chastity. I'll send him an email.

Elizabeth: Father LeBron? He's the priest who helped those models, Mark and Anna, write that St. Augustine book, right? The #1 bestseller in the non-fiction, Christian, Philosophy, Theology, self-help, and self-care/beauty genres, right? Wow, you think we could go and see him? The guy who helped models write a book that treated the City of God, the problem of evil, attachments, Protestants, time, and this, this conference theme, chastity?

Andrew: Yeah, that's him. You forgot to mention how jacked he is, though; a beast in the weight room, a monster. Apparently, he once got five atheists to convert and immediately enter the seminary because he picked up a car. It was like he had failed, over the course of a five hour coffeeshop conversation to convince them at all, they hadn't budged an inch from disbelief, and then he had them walk outside and he went under a random car, mechanic style, and just started bench pressing it.

Elizabeth: All five converted and entered the seminary?

Andrew: Yep. All have become excellent priests. One of them is an Archbishop somewhere in the Midwest. His motto pays homage to Father Lebron's evangelicalgifts. *Magnis Viribus, Vidi Veritas.* Do you know what that means?

Elizabeth: Yeah: 'By great strength, I saw the Truth.' . . . look, it says, 'GAME OVER: YOU WON.' What does that mean?

Andrew: It means 2025 is starting off on the right foot. Let's get out of here.

5. Donatism and Proto-Protestantism

Elizabeth: Hey, so what should we do about the lack of parking downtown?

Andrew: I think we should protest.

Elizabeth: No, I mean like actual solutions. Is there any kind of city planning authority we can appeal to?

Andrew: No. I just think we should protest.

Elizabeth: Wait... hold on... look, literally a few seconds of searching and I found the city planner's site and, look, excellent: a special submission box labeled, quote, 'let us know what we can do to make your daily life better.' Done, perfect.

Andrew: I'd rather just protest.

Elizabeth: You mean you don't want to fix the problem? Here's the solution. This city planner has the authority to fix this situation.

Andrew: Authority! Authority? What this guy he's like, what, he's like Vicar of City planning? He's like the Pontiff of Parking? This is stupid. Let's just protest instead. Let's protest loudly.

Elizabeth: That's not going to do anything. Plus, yeah, call him whatever you want, there's probably a reason he's head of this department.

Andrew: No, there's not. Every man is his own city planner. Just a man and his map, that's all you need.

Elizabeth: Then how come you and your 'every man is a city planner' friends have such different and irreconcilable differences about the same city map? It's the same map, but so many different opinions. They can't all be right. Remember your one friend, Ted? He literally said last week that according to his interpretation of Moscow's map, Moscow is actually in Vermont. And, if there's no authority to settle this, who's to say he's wrong?

Andrew: I still think we should protest. Loudly, with 'booming and thumping' awful music sung off key and with unimaginative lyrics but at least, silver lining, at least it really sucks too.

Elizabeth: I'm going to see the city planner. While I'm down there I'm going to enroll you in RCPIA—the Rite of City Planning Initiation for Adults. It's just what you and your friends need. And take heart: there's help, there's hope.

6. On Time and the Eternal Now

Elizabeth: Time waits for no man.

Andrew: Time flies when you're having fun.

Elizabeth: Time heals all wounds.

Andrew: Get with the times.

Elizabeth: A stitch in time saves nine.

Andrew: Time is money.

Elizabeth: The best time to start is now.

Andrew: In the nick of time.

Elizabeth: All in good time.

Andrew: So, remember that time, remember that time my boy, B-Money Smith, remember that time he was like, hey, check this out, and we were all like, no, no, dude, do not do that, but he was like I'm gonna, look, I'm gonna do it, I'm gonna do it now and then he did. And remember how much he regretted doing that later?

Elizabeth: I don't have time for that nonsense. I'm done.